JAPANESE-LANGUAGE PROFICIENCY TEST

Full N1-N5 Kanji Vocabulary List

Japanese - English - Croatian

Nihongo Tutors has been the most trusted tutoring institution in the area for over 3 years. We won't fail you!

日 (N5)	day, sun, Japan	dan
一 (N5)	one	jedan
国 (N5)	country	zemlja
人 (N5)	person	narod
年 (N5)	year	godina
大 (N5)	large, big	Velik
十 (N5)	ten	deset
二 (N5)	two	dva
本 (N5)	book, present, main, true, real	ovaj
中 (N5)	in, inside, middle, mean, center	u
長 (N5)	long, leader	dugo
出 (N5)	exit, leave	van
三 (N5)	three	tri
時 (N5)	time, hour	Vrijeme
行 (N5)	going, journey	Red
見 (N5)	see, hopes, chances, idea, opinion, look at, visible	vidjeti
月 (N5)	month, moon	mjesec
後 (N5)	behind, back, later	stražnji
前 (N5)	in front, before	prije
五 (N5)	five	fives

間 N5 interval, space između	**上** N5 above, up na	**東** N5 east istočno	**四** N5 four četiri
今 N5 now sada	**金** N5 gold zlato	**九** N5 nine devet	**入** N5 enter, insert Unesi
学 N5 study, learning, science studija	**高** N5 tall, high, expensive visok	**円** N5 circle, yen, round krug	**子** N5 child, sign of the rat, 11PM-1AM dijete
外 N5 outside izvan	**八** N5 eight osam	**六** N5 six šest	**下** N5 below, down, descend, give, low, inferior ispod
来 N5 come, due, next, cause, become doći	**気** N5 spirit, mind duh	**小** N5 little, small malo	**七** N5 seven sedam

山	話	女	北
N5	N5	N5	N5
mountain	tale, talk	woman, female	north
planina	priča	žena	sjeverno

午	百	書	先
N5	N5	N5	N5
noon, sign of the horse, 11AM-1PM	hundred	write	before, ahead, previous, future, precedence
podne	stotina	pisati	prije

名	川	千	水
N5	N5	N5	N5
name, noted, distinguished, reputation	stream, river	thousand	water
Ime	Rijeka	tisuću	voda

半	男	西	電
N5	N5	N5	N5
half, middle, odd number, semi-, part-half	male	west, Spain	electricity
pola	muški	Zapad	elektricitet

校	語	土	木
N5	N5	N5	N5
exam, school, printing, proof, correction	word, speech, language	soil, earth, ground, Turkey	tree, wood
ispit	govor	tlo	drvo

聞 N5	食 N5	車 N5	何 N5
hear, ask, listen	eat, food	car	what
čuti	jesti	automobil	što
南 N5	万 N5	毎 N5	白 N5
south	ten thousand	every	white
jug	deset tisuća	svaki	bijela
天 N5	母 N5	火 N5	右 N5
heavens, sky, imperial	mama, mother	fire	right
nebo	majka	vatra	pravo
読 N5	友 N5	左 N5	休 N5
read	friend	left	rest, day off, retire, sleep
čitati	prijatelj	lijevo	povući
父 N5	雨 N5	会 N5	同 N5
father	rain	meeting, meet, party, association, interview, join	same, agree, equal
otac	kiša	Zabava	složiti

事 N4	自 N4	社 N4	発 N4
matter, thing, fact, business, reason, possibly	oneself	company, firm, office, association, shrine	discharge, departure, publish, emit, start from
činjenica	sebe	društvo	pražnjenje
者 N4	地 N4	業 N4	方 N4
someone, person	ground, earth	business, vocation, arts, performance	direction, person, alternative
osoba	Zemlja	poslovanje	smjer
新 N4	場 N4	員 N4	立 N4
new	location, place	employee, member, number, the one in charge	stand up
novi	mjesto	zaposlenik	ustani
開 N4	手 N4	力 N4	問 N4
open, unfold, unseal	hand	power, strong, strain, bear up, exert	question, ask, problem
otvoren	ruka	sila	pitati
代 N4	明 N4	動 N4	京 N4
substitute, change, convert, replace, period	bright, light	move, motion, change, confusion, shift, shake	capital
generacija	Svijetao	pomicati	Peking

N4	N4	N4	N4
目	**通**	**言**	**理**
eye, class, look, insight, experience, care, favor	traffic, pass through, avenue, commute	say	logic, arrangement, reason, justice, truth
glava	kroz	Govor	Razlog
体	**田**	**主**	**題**
body, substance, object, reality, counter for images	rice field, rice paddy	lord, chief, master, main thing, principal	topic, subject
tijelo	polje	Gospodin	pitanje
意	**不**	**作**	**用**
idea, mind, heart, taste, thought, desire	negative, non-, bad, ugly, clumsy	make, production, prepare, build	utilize, business, service, use, employ
značenje	Nemoj	Napraviti	koristiti
度	**強**	**公**	**持**
degrees, occurrence, time, counter for occurrences	strong	public, prince, official, governmental	hold, have
stupanj	jak	javnost	Zadržavanje
野	**以**	**思**	**家**
plains, field, rustic, civilian life	by means of, because, in view of, compared with	think	house, home
divlji	Do	razmišljati	Obitelj

N4	N4	N4	N4
世 generation, world, society, public svijet	**多** many, frequent, much puno	**正** correct, justice, righteous, 10**40 pozitivan	**院** Inst., institution, temple, mansion, school bolnica
心 heart, mind, spirit srce	**界** world granica	**教** teach, faith, doctrine naučiti	**文** sentence, literature, style, art, decoration Tekst
元 beginning, former time, origin juan	**重** heavy, heap up, pile up, nest of boxes, -fold težina	**近** near, early, akin, tantamount blizu	**考** consider, think over test
画 brush-stroke, picture slikarstvo	**海** sea, ocean more	**売** sell prodati	**知** know, wisdom znati
道 road-way, street, district, journey, course cesta	**集** gather, meet, congregate, swarm, flock okupiti	**別** separate, branch off, diverge, fork, another odvojen	**物** thing, object, matter objekt

使 N4 use koristiti	**品** N4 goods, refinement, dignity, article Proizvod	**計** N4 plot, plan, scheme, measure shema	**死** N4 death, die mrtav
特 N4 special poseban	**私** N4 private, I, me privatna	**始** N4 commence, begin početak	**朝** N4 morning, dynasty, regime, epoch, period za
運 N4 carry, luck, destiny, fate, lot, transport Prijevoz	**終** N4 end, finish kraj	**台** N4 pedestal, a stand, counter for machines and vehicles stanica	**広** N4 wide, broad, spacious širok
住 N4 dwell, reside, live, inhabit stanovati	**真** N4 true, reality, Buddhist sect stvarnost	**有** N4 possess, have, exist, happen, occur, approx posjedovati	**口** N4 mouth usta
少 N4 few, little manje	**町** N4 village, town, block, street selo	**料** N4 fee, materials materijal	**工** N4 craft, construction čamac

N4	N4	N4	N4
建	空	急	止
build	empty, sky, void, vacant, vacuum	hurry, emergency, sudden, steep	stop, halt
izgraditi	nebo	žuriti	Stop
送	切	転	研
escort, send	cut, cutoff, be sharp	revolve, turn around, change	polish, study of, sharpen
pratnja	odrezati	smjenjivati	istraživanje
足	究	楽	起
leg, foot, be sufficient	research, study	music, comfort, ease	rouse, wake up, get up
noga	studija	glazba, muzika	probudi se
着	店	病	質
arrive, wear, counter for suits of clothing	store, shop	ill, sick	substance, quality, matter, temperament
stići	trgovinama	bolestan	kvaliteta
待	試	族	銀
wait, depend on	test, try, attempt, experiment, ordeal	tribe, family	silver
Čekati	test	Obitelj	srebro

N4	N4	N4	N4
早 early, fast rano	映 reflect, reflection, projection odraziti	親 parent, intimacy, relative, familiarity roditelj	験 verification, effect, testing utjecaj
英 England, English Engleski	医 doctor, medicine medicinski	仕 attend, doing, official, serve službeno	去 gone, past, quit, leave, elapse, eliminate, divorce prestati
味 flavor, taste ukus	写 copy, be photographed, describe kopirati	字 character, letter, word, section of village lik	答 solution, answer odgovor
夜 night, evening noć	音 sound, noise zvuk	注 pour, irrigate, shed (tears), flow into navodnjavati	帰 homecoming, arrive at, lead to, result in povratak kući
古 old drevni	歌 song, sing pjesma	買 buy kupiti	悪 bad, vice, rascal, false, evil, wrong loše

図 (N4)	map, drawing, plan, unexpected, accidentally	Karte
週 (N4)	week	tjedan
室 (N4)	room, apartment, chamber, greenhouse, cellar	soba
歩 (N4)	walk, counter for steps	hodati
風 (N4)	wind, air, style, manner	vjetar
紙 (N4)	paper	papir
黒 (N4)	black	Crno
花 (N4)	flower	cvijet
春 (N4)	springtime, spring (season)	Proljeće
赤 (N4)	red	Crvena
青 (N4)	blue, green	zelena
館 (N4)	building, mansion, large building, palace	zgrada
屋 (N4)	roof, house, shop, dealer, seller	kuća
色 (N4)	color	boja
走 (N4)	run	trčanje
秋 (N4)	autumn	jesen
夏 (N4)	summer	ljeto
習 (N4)	learn	studija
駅 (N4)	station	stanica
洋 (N4)	ocean, western style	ocean

旅 N4	服 N4	夕 N4	借 N4
trip, travel	clothing, admit, obey, discharge	evening	borrow, rent
putovati	odjeća	večer	posuditi
曜 N4	飲 N4	肉 N4	貸 N4
weekday	drink, smoke, take	meat	lend
radni dan	piće	meso	posuditi
堂 N4	鳥 N4	飯 N4	勉 N4
public chamber, hall	bird, chicken	meal, boiled rice	exertion
dvorana	ptica	riža	napor
冬 N4	昼 N4	茶 N4	牛 N4
winter	daytime, noon	tea	cow
zima	dan	čaj	krava
魚 N4	兄 N4	犬 N4	漢 N4
fish	elder brother, big brother	dog	Sino-, China
riba	Brat	pas	kineski

政 (N3) politics, government Vlada	**議** (N3) deliberation, consultation, debate, consideration raspravljati	**民** (N3) people, nation, subjects narod	**連** (N3) take along, lead, join, connect, party, gang, clique pridružiti
対 (N3) vis-a-vis, opposite, even, equal, versus, anti- suprotan	**部** (N3) section, bureau, dept, class, copy, part odjeljak	**合** (N3) fit, suit, join odijelo	**市** (N3) market, city, town Grad
内 (N3) inside, within, between, among, house, home Iznutra	**相** (N3) inter-, mutual, together, each other zajedno	**定** (N3) determine, fix, establish, decide uspostaviti	**回** (N3) -times, round, game, revolve smjenjivati
選 (N3) elect, select, choose, prefer izabrati	**米** (N3) rice, USA, metre Metar	**実** (N3) reality, truth istina	**関** (N3) connection, barrier, gateway, involve, concerning prepreka
決 (N3) decide, fix, agree upon, appoint Odlučiti	**全** (N3) whole, entire, all, complete, fulfill svi	**表** (N3) surface, table, chart, diagram stol	**戦** (N3) war, battle, match bitka

N3 **経** sutra, longitude, pass thru, expire, warp isteći	**N3** **最** utmost, most, extreme najviše	**N3** **現** present, existing, actual Predstaviti	**N3** **調** tune, tone, meter, key (music), writing style napjev
N3 **化** change, take the form of, influence, enchant promijeniti	**N3** **当** hit, right, appropriate, himself pogoditi	**N3** **約** promise, approximately, shrink približno	**N3** **首** neck vrat
N3 **法** method, law, rule, principle, model, system zakon	**N3** **性** sex, gender, nature rod	**N3** **要** need, main point, essence, pivot, key to potreba	**N3** **制** system, law, rule sustav
N3 **治** reign, be at peace, calm down, subdue, quell vladavina	**N3** **務** task, duties zadatak	**N3** **成** turn into, become, get, grow, elapse, reach postati	**N3** **期** period, time, date, term razdoblje
N3 **取** take, fetch, take up donijeti	**N3** **都** metropolis, capital glavni	**N3** **和** harmony, Japanese style, peace, soften, Japan sklad	**N3** **機** mechanism, opportunity, occasion, machine, airplane mašina

平 N3	加 N3	受 N3	続 N3
even, flat, peace	add, addition, increase, join, include, Canada	accept, undergo, answer (phone), take, get	continue, series, sequel
nivo	dodatak	Prihvatiti	nastaviti
進 N3	数 N3	記 N3	初 N3
advance, proceed, progress, promote	number, strength, fate, law, figures	scribe, account, narrative	first time, beginning
unaprijed	broj	pisar	rano
指 N3	権 N3	支 N3	産 N3
finger, point to, indicate, put into, play (chess)	authority, power, rights	branch, support, sustain	products, bear, give birth, yield, childbirth
naznačiti	vlast	podrška	Proizvodimo
点 N3	報 N3	済 N3	活 N3
spot, point, mark, speck, decimal point	report, news, reward, retribution	finish, come to an end, excusable, need not	lively, resuscitation, being helped, living
točka	izvješće	Završi	živo
原 N3	共 N3	得 N3	解 N3
meadow, original, primitive, field, plain	together, both, neither, all, and, alike, with	gain, get, find, earn, acquire, can, may	unravel, notes, key, explanation
izvornik	zajedno	dobit	riješenje

交 (N3)	資 (N3)	予 (N3)	向 (N3)
mingle, mixing, association, coming & going	assets, resources, capital, funds, data	beforehand, previous, myself, I	yonder, facing, beyond, confront, defy
asocijacija	resursi	unaprijed	Iznad
際 (N3)	勝 (N3)	面 (N3)	告 (N3)
occasion, side, edge, verge, dangerous, adventurous	victory, win, prevail, excel	mask, face, features, surface	revelation, tell, inform, announce
prilika	Pobijediti	površinski	najaviti
反 (N3)	判 (N3)	認 (N3)	参 (N3)
anti-	judgement, signature, stamp, seal	acknowledge, witness, discern, recognize	nonplussed, three, going, coming, visiting
anti-	osuda	prepoznati	Sudjelovati
利 (N3)	組 (N3)	信 (N3)	在 (N3)
profit, advantage, benefit	association, braid, plait, construct, assemble	faith, truth, fidelity, trust	exist, outskirts, suburbs, located in
Profit	asocijacija	vjera	postojati
件 (N3)	側 (N3)	任 (N3)	引 (N3)
affair, case, matter, item	side, lean, oppose, regret	responsibility, duty, term, entrust to, appoint	pull, tug, jerk, admit, install, quote, refer to
afera	strana	odgovornost	Vuci

N3	N3	N3	N3
求	所	次	昨
request, want, wish for, require, demand	place	next, order, sequence	yesterday, previous
zahtjev	mjesto	sekvenca	Jučer
論	官	増	係
argument, discourse	bureaucrat, the government	increase, add, augment, gain, promote	person in charge, connection, duty, concern oneself
argument	birokrata	povećati	dužnost
感	情	投	示
emotion, feeling, sensation	feelings, emotion, passion, sympathy	throw, discard, abandon, launch into, join	show, indicate, point out, express, display
emocija	osjećaji	odbaciti	naznačiti
変	打	直	両
unusual, change, strange	strike, hit, knock, pound, dozen	straightaway, honesty, frankness, fix, repair	both, old Japanese coin, counter for vehicles, two
čudan	štrajk	poštenje	oba
式	確	果	容
style, ceremony, rite, function, method, system	assurance, firm, tight, hard, solid, confirm	fruit, reward, carry out, achieve, complete, end	contain, form, looks
ceremonija	uvjerenje	voće	sadržati

必 (N3)	演 (N3)	歳 (N3)	争 (N3)
invariably, certain, inevitable	performance, act, play, render, stage	year-end, age, occasion, opportunity	contend, dispute, argue
neizbježan	izvođenje	prilika	rasprava
談 (N3)	能 (N3)	位 (N3)	置 (N3)
discuss, talk	ability, talent, skill, capacity	rank, grade, throne, crown, about, some	placement, put, set, deposit, leave behind
razgovor	vještina	rang	plasman
流 (N3)	格 (N3)	疑 (N3)	過 (N3)
current, a sink, flow, forfeit	status, rank, capacity, character	doubt, distrust, be suspicious, question	overdo, exceed, go beyond, error
Trenutno	status	sumnjiv	prekoračiti
局 (N3)	放 (N3)	常 (N3)	状 (N3)
bureau, board, office, affair, conclusion	set free, release, fire, shoot, emit, banish	usual, ordinary, normal, regular	status quo, conditions, circumstances, form
biro	puštanje	običan	okolnosti
球 (N3)	職 (N3)	与 (N3)	供 (N3)
ball, sphere	post, employment, work	bestow, participate in, give, award, impart, provide	submit, offer, present, serve (meal), accompany
lopta	Posao	protiv	podnijeti

N3	N3	N3	N3
役	**構**	**割**	**費**
duty, war, campaign, drafted labor, office, service	posture, build, pretend	proportion, comparatively, divide, cut, separate	expense, cost, spend, consume, waste
dužnost	držanje	razmjer	trošak
付	**由**	**説**	**難**
adhere, attach, refer to, append	wherefore, a reason	rumor, opinion, theory	difficult, impossible, trouble, accident, defect
Pridržavajte	razlog	glasina	težak
優	**夫**	**収**	**断**
tenderness, excel, surpass, actor, superiority	husband, man	income, obtain, reap, pay, supply, store	severance, decline, refuse, apologize
izvrstan	suprug	prihod	prekid
石	**違**	**消**	**神**
stone	difference, differ	extinguish, blow out, turn off, neutralize, cancel	gods, mind, soul
kamen	razlika	ugasiti	Bog
番	**規**	**術**	**備**
turn, number in a series	standard, measure	art, technique, skill, means, trick, resources	equip, provision, preparation
skretanje	standard	Tehnika	Pripremiti

宅 N3	害 N3	配 N3	警 N3
home, house, residence, our house, my husband	harm, injury	distribute, spouse, exile, rationing	admonish, commandment
Kuća	šteta	raspodijeliti	opominjati
育 N3	席 N3	訪 N3	乗 N3
bring up, grow up, raise, rear	seat, mat, occasion, place	call on, visit, look up, offer sympathy	ride, power, multiplication, record
podići	sjedalo	posjetiti	Pomnožiti
残 N3	想 N3	声 N3	念 N3
remainder, leftover, balance	concept, think, idea, thought	voice	wish, sense, idea, thought, feeling, desire
ostatak	koncept	zvuk	želja
助 N3	労 N3	例 N3	然 N3
help, rescue, assist	labor, thank for, reward for, toil, trouble	example, custom, usage, precedent	sort of thing, so, if so, in that case, well
Pomozite	rad	primjer	Naravno
限 N3	追 N3	商 N3	葉 N3
limit, restrict, to best of ability	chase, drive away, follow, pursue, meanwhile	make a deal, selling, dealing in, merchant	leaf, plane, lobe, needle, blade, spear
ograničiti	loviti	trgovac	list

伝 (N3) transmit, go along, walk along, follow, report prenositi	**働** (N3) work, (kokuji) Raditi	**形** (N3) shape, form, style oblik	**景** (N3) scenery, view dekoracije
好 (N3) fond, pleasing, like something prijatan	**退** (N3) retreat, withdraw, retire, resign, repel, expel Povlačenje	**頭** (N3) head, counter for large animals glava	**負** (N3) defeat, negative, -, minus, bear, owe negativan
渡 (N3) transit, ford, ferry, cross, import, deliver tranzit	**失** (N3) lose, error, fault, disadvantage, loss Gubitak	**差** (N3) distinction, difference, variation, discrepancy razlika	**末** (N3) end, close, tip, powder, posterity Kraj
守 (N3) guard, protect, defend, obey odbrana	**若** (N3) young, if, perhaps, possibly, low number, immature mladi	**種** (N3) species, kind, class, variety, seed sjeme	**美** (N3) beauty, beautiful Ljepota
命 (N3) fate, command, decree, destiny, life, appoint život	**福** (N3) blessing, fortune, luck, wealth blagoslov	**望** (N3) ambition, full moon, hope, desire, aspire to, expect ambicija	**非** (N3) un-, mistake, negative, injustice, non- pogreška

N3	N3	N3	N3
観 outlook, look, appearance, condition, view izgled	**察** guess, presume, surmise, judge, understand nagađati	**段** grade, steps, stairs Korak	**横** sideways, side, horizontal, width, woof strana
深 deep, heighten, intensify, strengthen Duboko	**申** have the honor to, sign of the monkey, 3-5PM Majmun	**様** Esq., way, manner, situation, polite suffix situacija	**財** property, money, wealth, assets bogatstvo
港 harbor luka	**識** discriminating, know, write diskriminirati	**呼** call, call out to, invite pozvati	**達** accomplished, reach, arrive, attain ostvariti
良 good, pleasing, skilled Dobro	**候** climate, season, weather Vrijeme	**程** extent, degree, law, formula, distance, limits opseg	**満** full, enough, pride, satisfy puni
敗 failure, defeat, reversal Poraz	**値** price, cost, value vrijednost	**光** ray, light zraka	**路** path, route, road, distance put

N3	N3	N3	N3
科	積	他	処
department, course, section	volume, product (x*y), acreage, contents, pile up	other, another, the others	dispose, manage, deal with, sentence, condemn
odjel	svezak	drugo	raspolagati

N3	N3	N3	N3
太	客	否	師
plump, thick, big around	guest, visitor, customer, client	negate, no, noes, refuse, decline, deny	expert, teacher, master, army, war
gust	Gost	negirati	stručnjak

N3	N3	N3	N3
登	易	速	存
ascend, climb up	easy, ready to, simple, fortune-telling, divination	quick, fast	suppose, be aware of, believe, feel
Uspon	Lako	ubrzati	pretpostaviti

N3	N3	N3	N3
飛	殺	号	単
fly, skip (pages), scatter	kill, murder, butcher, slice off, split, diminish	nickname, number, item, title, pseudonym, name, call	simple, one, single, merely
letjeti	ubiti	nadimak	jednostavan

N3	N3	N3	N3
座	破	除	完
squat, seat, cushion, gathering, sit	rend, rip, tear, break, destroy, defeat, frustrate	exclude, division (x, 3), remove, abolish, cancel	perfect, completion, end
sjedalo	slomljen	osim	savršen

N3	N3	N3	N3
降	責	捕	危
descend, precipitate, fall, surrender	blame, condemn, censure	catch, capture	dangerous, fear, uneasy
sići	krivica	ulov	opasno
給	苦	迎	園
salary, wage, gift, allow, grant, bestow on	suffering, trial, worry, hardship, feel bitter	welcome, meet, greet	park, garden, yard, farm
plaća	pati	Dobrodošli	vrt
具	辞	因	馬
tool, utensil, means, possess, ingredients	resign, word, term, expression	cause, factor, be associated with, depend on	horse
alatka	dati ostavku	jer	konj
愛	富	彼	未
love, affection, favourite	wealth, enrich, abundant	he, that, the	un-, not yet, hitherto, still, even now
Ljubav	obilan	on	ne
舞	亡	冷	適
dance, flit, circle, wheel	deceased, the late, dying, perish	cool, cold (beer, person), chill	suitable, occasional, rare, qualified, capable
ples	pokojni	jeza	prikladan

婦 N3 lady, woman, wife, bride žena	**寄** N3 draw near, stop in, bring near, gather, collect poslati
込 N3 crowded, mixture, in bulk, included gužva	**顔** N3 face, expression izraz
類 N3 sort, kind, variety, class, genus klasa	**余** N3 too much, myself, surplus, other, remainder sebe
王 N3 king, rule, magnate kralj	**返** N3 return, answer, fade, repay povratak
妻 N3 wife, spouse žena	**背** N3 stature, height, back, behind, disobey, defy stas
熱 N3 heat, temperature, fever, mania, passion toplina	**宿** N3 inn, lodging, relay station, dwell, lodge gostionica
薬 N3 medicine, chemical, enamel, gunpowder, benefit lijek	**頼** N3 trust, request povjerenje
覚 N3 memorize, learn, remember, awake, sober up Zapamtite	**船** N3 ship, boat trajekt
途 N3 route, way, road put	**許** N3 permit, approve odobriti
抜 N3 slip out, extract, pull out, pilfer, quote, remove ekstrakt	**便** N3 convenience pogodnost

N3	N3	N3	N3
留	**罪**	**努**	**精**
detain, fasten, halt, stop	guilt, sin, crime, fault, blame, offense	toil, diligent, as much as possible	refined, ghost, fairy, energy, vitality, semen
uhitila	kriminal	marljiv	profinjen
N3	N3	N3	N3
散	**静**	**婚**	**喜**
scatter, disperse, spend, squander	quiet	marriage	rejoice, take pleasure in
raspršiti	Miran	brak	Raduj
N3	N3	N3	N3
浮	**絶**	**幸**	**押**
floating, float, rise to surface	discontinue, beyond, sever, cut off, abstain	happiness, blessing, fortune	push, stop, check, subdue, attach
plutati	obustaviti	sreća	gurnuti
N3	N3	N3	N3
倒	**老**	**曲**	**払**
overthrow, fall, collapse, drop, break down	old man, old age, grow old	bend, music, melody, composition	pay, clear out, prune, banish, dispose of
svrgnuti	star	glazba, muzika	platiti
N3	N3	N3	N3
庭	**徒**	**勤**	**遅**
courtyard, garden, yard	junior, emptiness, vanity, futility, uselessness	diligence, become employed, serve	slow, late, back, later
dvorište	mlađi	Marljivost	usporiti

居 N3	雑 N3	招 N3	困 N3
reside, to be, exist, live with	miscellaneous	beckon, invite, summon, engage	quandary, become distressed, annoyed
prebivati	razni	dati znak	ojađen
刻 N3	賛 N3	抱 N3	犯 N3
engrave, cut fine, chop, hash, mince, time, carving	approve, praise, title or inscription on picture	embrace, hug, hold in arms	crime, sin, offense
urezani	odobriti	zagrljaj	kriminal
恐 N3	息 N3	遠 N3	戻 N3
fear, dread, awe	breath, respiration, son, interest (on money)	distant, far	re-, return, revert, resume, restore, go backwards
strah	dah	udaljen	povratak
願 N3	絵 N3	越 N3	欲 N3
petition, request, vow, wish, hope	picture, drawing, painting, sketch	surpass, cross over, move to, exceed, Vietnam	longing, covetousness, greed, passion, desire
peticija	slika	nadmašiti	strast
痛 N3	笑 N3	互 N3	束 N3
pain, hurt, damage, bruise	laugh	mutually, reciprocally, together	bundle, sheaf, ream, tie in bundles, govern
bol	smijeh	zajednički	paket

似 N3	列 N3	探 N3	逃 N3
becoming, resemble, counterfeit, imitate, suitable	file, row, rank, tier, column	grope, search, look for	escape, flee, shirk, evade, set free
ličiti	Stupac	Istražiti	pobjeći
遊 N3	迷 N3	夢 N3	君 N3
play	astray, be perplexed, in doubt, lost, err, illusion	dream, vision, illusion	old boy, name-suffix
obilazak	pogrešnim putem	san	stari dečko
閉 N3	緒 N3	折 N3	草 N3
closed, shut	thong, beginning, inception, end, cord, strap	fold, break, fracture, bend, yield, submit	grass, weeds, herbs, pasture, write, draft
Zatvoriti	početak	preklopiti	trava
暮 N3	酒 N3	悲 N3	晴 N3
livelihood, make a living, spend time	sake, alcohol	jail cell, grieve, sad, deplore, regret	clear up
izdržavanje	liker	tužan	čisto
掛 N3	到 N3	寝 N3	暗 N3
hang, suspend, depend, arrive at, tax, pour	arrival, proceed, reach, attain, result in	lie down, sleep, rest, bed, remain unsold	darkness, disappear, shade, informal
objesiti	dolazak	spavati	tama

盗 N3	吸 N3	陽 N3	御 N3
steal, rob, pilfer	suck, imbibe, inhale, sip	sunshine, yang principle, positive, male, heaven	honorable, manipulate, govern
Ukrasti	udisati	sunce	častan
歯 N3	忘 N3	雪 N3	吹 N3
tooth, cog	forget	snow	blow, breathe, puff, emit, smoke
zub	zaboraviti	snijeg	udarac
娘 N3	誤 N3	洗 N3	慣 N3
daughter, girl	mistake, err, do wrong, mislead	wash, inquire into, probe	accustomed, get used to, become experienced
kći	greška	pranje	navikao
礼 N3	窓 N3	昔 N3	貧 N3
salute, bow, ceremony, thanks, remuneration	window, pane	once upon a time, antiquity, old times	poverty, poor
ceremonija	prozor	antika	siromaštvo
怒 N3	泳 N3	祖 N3	杯 N3
angry, be offended	swim	ancestor, pioneer, founder	counter for cupfuls, wine glass, glass, toast
ljut	plivanje	Predak	šalice

疲 N3 exhausted, tire, weary iscrpljena	**皆** N3 all, everything sve	**腹** N3 abdomen, belly, stomach trbuh	**煙** N3 smoke dim
眠 N3 sleep, die, sleepy spavati	**怖** N3 dreadful, be frightened, fearful teror	**耳** N3 ear uho	**頂** N3 place on the head, receive, top of head, top, summit vrh
箱 N3 box, chest, case, bin, railway car kutija	**晩** N3 nightfall, night sumrak	**寒** N3 cold hladno	**髪** N3 hair of the head dlaka
忙 N3 busy, occupied, restless zaposlen	**才** N3 genius, years old, cubic shaku genije	**靴** N3 shoes cipele	**恥** N3 shame, dishonor sramota
偶 N3 accidentally, even number, couple, man & wife slučajno	**偉** N3 admirable, greatness, remarkable, conceited izvrstan	**猫** N3 cat Mačka	**幾** N3 how many, how much, how far, how long koliko

党 N2	協 N2	総 N2	区 N2
party, faction, clique	co-, cooperation	general, whole, all, full, total	ward, district
Zabava	suradnja	Općenito	okrug
領 N2	県 N2	設 N2	改 N2
jurisdiction, dominion, territory, fief, reign	prefecture	establishment, provision, prepare	reformation, change, modify, mend, renew
vlast	Prefektura	osnivanje	reformacija
府 N2	査 N2	委 N2	軍 N2
borough, urban prefecture, govt office	investigate	committee, entrust to, leave to, devote, discard	army, force, troops, war, battle
Kuća	istraga	odbor	vojni
団 N2	各 N2	島 N2	革 N2
group, association	each, every, either	island	leather, become serious, skin, hide, pelt
skupina	svaki	otoka	koža
村 N2	勢 N2	減 N2	再 N2
town, village	forces, energy, military strength	dwindle, decrease, reduce, decline, curtail	again, twice, second time
selo	snaga	splasnuti	opet

税 **N2**	営 **N2**	比 **N2**	防 **N2**
tax, duty	occupation, camp, perform, build, conduct (business)	compare, race, ratio, Philipines	ward off, defend, protect, resist
porez	okupacija	usporediti	zaštititi
補 **N2**	境 **N2**	導 **N2**	副 **N2**
supplement, supply, make good, offset, compensate	boundary, border, region	guidance, leading, conduct, usher	vice-, duplicate, copy
dopuniti	granica	vođenje	duplikat
算 **N2**	輸 **N2**	述 **N2**	線 **N2**
calculate, divining, number, abacus, probability	transport, send, be inferior	mention, state, speak, relate	line, track
izračunati	prijevoz	spomenuti	crta
農 **N2**	州 **N2**	武 **N2**	象 **N2**
agriculture, farmers	state, province	warrior, military, chivalry, arms	elephant, pattern after, imitate, image, shape
poljoprivreda	pokrajina	ratnik	Slon
域 **N2**	額 **N2**	欧 **N2**	担 **N2**
range, region, limits, stage, level	forehead, tablet, plaque, framed picture, sum	Europe	shouldering, carry, raise, bear
područje	čelo	Europa	shouldering

準
N2

semi-, correspond to, proportionate to, conform

odgovara

賞
N2

prize, reward, praise

nagrada

辺
N2

environs, boundary, border, vicinity

granica

造
N2

create, make, structure, physique

stvoriti

被
N2

incur, cover, veil, brood over, shelter, wear

napraviti

技
N2

skill, art, craft, ability, feat, performance

Vještina

低
N2

lower, short, humble

nizak

復
N2

restore, return to, revert, resume

vratiti

移
N2

shift, move, change, drift, catch (cold, fire)

smjena

個
N2

individual, counter for articles and military units

pojedinac

門
N2

gates

vrata

課
N2

chapter, lesson, section, department, division

lekcija

脳
N2

brain, memory

mozak

極
N2

poles, settlement, conclusion, end

pol

含
N2

include, bear in mind, understand, cherish

uključiti

蔵
N2

storehouse, hide, own, have, possess

skladište

量
N2

quantity, measure, weight, amount, consider

količina

型
N2

mould, type, model

kalup

況
N2

condition, situation

stanje

針
N2

needle, pin, staple, stinger

igla

専 N2 specialty, exclusive, mainly, solely specijalitet	**谷** N2 valley Dolina	**史** N2 history, chronicle povijest	**階** N2 storey, stair, counter for storeys of a building kat
管 N2 pipe, tube, wind instrument, drunken talk cijev	**兵** N2 soldier, private, troops, army, warfare, strategy Vojnik	**接** N2 touch, contact, adjoin, piece together dodir	**細** N2 dainty, get thin, taper, slender, narrow poslastica
効 N2 merit, efficacy, efficiency, benefit zasluga	**丸** N2 round, full, month, perfection, -ship, pills krug	**湾** N2 gulf, bay, inlet Zaljev	**録** N2 record snimiti
省 N2 focus, government ministry, conserve usredotočenost	**橋** N2 bridge most	**岸** N2 beach poduprijeti	**周** N2 circumference, circuit, lap opseg
材 N2 lumber, log, timber, wood, talent drvo	**戸** N2 door vrata	**央** N2 center, middle centar	**券** N2 ticket ulaznica

編 N2	捜 N2	竹 N2	並 N2
compilation, knit, plait, braid, twist, editing	search, look for, locate	bamboo	row, and, besides, as well as, line up, rank with
kompilacija	traži	bambus	osim
療 N2	採 N2	森 N2	競 N2
heal, cure	pick, take, fetch, take up	forest, woods	emulate, compete with, bid, sell at auction
liječiti	Odabrati	šuma	Emulate
介 N2	根 N2	販 N2	歴 N2
jammed in, shellfish, mediate, concern oneself with	root, radical, head (pimple)	marketing, sell, trade	curriculum, continuation, passage of time
školjka	korijen	Marketing	nastavni plan
将 N2	幅 N2	般 N2	貿 N2
leader, commander, general, admiral, or	hanging scroll, width	carrier, carry, all	trade, exchange
lider	Širina	nosač	trgovina
講 N2	林 N2	装 N2	諸 N2
lecture, club, association	grove, forest	attire, dress, pretend, disguise, profess	various, many, several, together
predavanje	šuma	ruho	raznovrstan

劇 N2	河 N2	航 N2	鉄 N2
drama, play	river	navigate, sail, cruise, fly	iron
drama	Rijeka	navigaciju	željezo
児 N2	禁 N2	印 N2	逆 N2
newborn babe, child, young of animals	prohibition, ban, forbid	stamp, seal, mark, imprint, symbol, emblem	inverted, reverse, opposite, wicked
pedijatrijski	zabrana	Pečat	inverzan
換 N2	久 N2	短 N2	油 N2
interchange, period, charge, change?	long time, old story	short, brevity, fault, defect, weak point	oil, fat
promijeniti	Dugo vrijeme	kratkoća	ulje
暴 N2	輪 N2	占 N2	植 N2
outburst, rave, fret, force, violence, cruelty	wheel, ring, circle, link, loop	fortune-telling, divining, forecasting, occupy	plant
nasilan	kotač	proricanje	biljka
清 N2	倍 N2	均 N2	億 N2
pure, purify, cleanse, exorcise, Manchu dynasty	double, twice, times, fold	level, average	hundred million
čist	dvostruko	nivo	milijardi

圧 N2	芸 N2	署 N2	伸 N2
pressure, push, overwhelm, oppress, dominate	technique, art, craft, performance, acting	signature, govt office, police station	expand, stretch, extend, lengthen, increase
pritisak	tehnika	potpis	rastezanje
停 N2	爆 N2	陸 N2	玉 N2
halt, stopping	bomb, burst open, pop, split	land, six	jewel, ball
zaustaviti	prasak	zemljište	dragulj
波 N2	帯 N2	延 N2	羽 N2
waves, billows, Poland	sash, belt, obi, zone, region	prolong, stretching	feathers, counter for birds, rabbits
val	pojas	produžiti	pero
固 N2	則 N2	乱 N2	普 N2
harden, set, clot, curdle	rule, follow, based on, model after	riot, war, disorder, disturb	universal, wide(ly), generally, Prussia
solidan	Pravilo	poremećaj	Općenito
測 N2	豊 N2	厚 N2	齢 N2
fathom, plan, scheme, measure	bountiful, excellent, rich	thick, heavy, rich, kind, cordial, brazen, shameless	age
shema	izvrstan	gust	dob

囲 N2 surround, besiege, store, paling, enclosure Surround	**卒** N2 graduate, soldier, private, die diplomirani	**略** N2 abbreviation, omission, outline, shorten, capture skraćenica	**承** N2 acquiesce, hear, listen to, be informed, receive prešutna saglasnost
順 N2 obey, order, turn, right, docility, occasion slušate	**岩** N2 boulder, rock, cliff stijena	**練** N2 practice, gloss, train, drill, polish, refine praksa	**軽** N2 lightly, trifling, unimportant olako
了 N2 complete, finish Završi	**庁** N2 government office vladin ured	**城** N2 castle dvorac	**患** N2 afflicted, disease, suffer from, be ill Patiti
層 N2 stratum, social class, layer, story, floor sloj	**版** N2 printing block, printing plate, edition, impression označiti	**令** N2 orders, ancient laws, command, decree naredba	**角** N2 angle, corner, square, horn, antlers kut
絡 N2 entwine, coil around, get caught in uplesti	**損** N2 damage, loss, disadvantage, hurt, injure šteta	**募** N2 recruit, campaign, gather (contributions) Novak	**裏** N2 back, amidst, in, reverse, inside, palm, sole usred

N2	N2	N2	N2
仏	績	築	貨
Buddha, the dead, France	exploits, unreeling cocoons	fabricate, build, construct	freight, goods, property
Buda	eksploatira	izmišljati	teretni
N2	**N2**	**N2**	**N2**
混	昇	池	血
mix, blend, confuse	rise up	pond, cistern, pool, reservoir	blood
mješavina	Ustati	Bazen	krv
N2	**N2**	**N2**	**N2**
温	季	星	永
warm	seasons	star, spot, dot, mark	eternity, long, lengthy
toplo	sezona	zvijezda	Zauvijek
N2	**N2**	**N2**	**N2**
著	誌	庫	刊
renowned, publish, write, remarkable	document, records	warehouse, storehouse	publish, carve, engrave
slavan	dokument	skladište	objaviti
N2	**N2**	**N2**	**N2**
像	香	坂	底
statue, picture, image, figure, portrait	incense, smell, perfume	slope, incline, hill	bottom, sole, depth, bottom price, base, kind, sort
slika	tamjan	nagib	dno

布	寺	宇	巨
N2	N2	N2	N2
linen, cloth	Buddhist temple	eaves, roof, house, heaven	gigantic, big, large, great
tkanina	hram	krov	ogroman

震	希	触	依
N2	N2	N2	N2
quake, shake, tremble, quiver, shiver	hope, beg, request, pray, beseech, Greece	contact, touch, feel, hit, proclaim, announce	reliant, depend on, consequently, therefore, due to
potresti	nada	dodir	prema

籍	汚	枚	複
N2	N2	N2	N2
enroll, domiciliary register, membership	dirty, pollute, disgrace, rape, defile	sheet of..., counter for flat thin objects or sheets	duplicate, double, compound, multiple
upisati	prljav	listovi	kompleks

郵	仲	栄	札
N2	N2	N2	N2
mail, stagecoach stop	go-between, relationship	flourish, prosperity, honor, glory, splendor	tag, paper money, counter for bonds, placard, bid
pošta	odnos	procvjetati	označiti

板	骨	傾	届
N2	N2	N2	N2
plank, board, plate, stage	skeleton, bone, remains, frame	lean, incline, tilt, trend, wane, sink, ruin, bias	deliver, reach, arrive, report, notify, forward
daska	kost	sipati	dostaviti

巻 N2 scroll, volume, book, part, roll up Svezak	**燃** N2 burn, blaze, glow spaliti	**跡** N2 tracks, mark, print, impression trag	**包** N2 wrap, pack up, cover, conceal paket
駐 N2 stop-over, reside in, resident Stanica	**弱** N2 weak, frail slab	**紹** N2 introduce, inherit, help predstaviti	**雇** N2 employ, hire najam
替 N2 exchange, spare, substitute, per- razmjena	**預** N2 deposit, custody, leave with, entrust to depozit	**焼** N2 bake, burning peći	**簡** N2 simplicity, brevity jednostavan
章 N2 badge, chapter, composition, poem, design Bedž	**臓** N2 entrails, viscera, bowels iznutrice	**律** N2 rhythm, law, regulation, gauge, control ritam	**贈** N2 presents, send, give to, award to, confer on predstavlja
照 N2 illuminate, shine, compare, bashful sjaj	**薄** N2 dilute, thin, weak (tea) tanak	**群** N2 flock, group, crowd, herd, swarm, cluster skupina	**奥** N2 heart, interior srce

詰 N2 packed, close, pressed, reprove, rebuke, blame grditi	**双** N2 pair, set, comparison, counter for pairs dvostruko	**刺** N2 thorn, pierce, stab, prick, sting, calling card trn	**純** N2 genuine, purity, innocence, net (profit) čist
翌 N2 the following, next Sljedeći	**快** N2 cheerful, pleasant, agreeable, comfortable veseo	**片** N2 one-sided, leaf, sheet list	**敬** N2 awe, respect, honor, revere S poštovanjem
悩 N2 trouble, worry, in pain, distress, illness nevolja	**泉** N2 spring, fountain Proljeće	**皮** N2 pelt, skin, hide, leather koža	**漁** N2 fishing, fishery ribarstvo
荒 N2 laid waste, rough, rude, wild nepristojan	**貯** N2 savings, store, lay in, keep, wear mustache štednja	**硬** N2 stiff, hard teško	**埋** N2 bury, be filled up, embedded pokopati
柱 N2 pillar, post, cylinder, support stub	**祭** N2 ritual, offer prayers, celebrate, deify ritual	**袋** N2 sack, bag, pouch torba	**筆** N2 writing brush, writing, painting brush, handwriting slikarski kist

訓 N2	浴 N2	童 N2	宝 N2
instruction, Japanese character reading	bathe, be favored with, bask in	juvenile, child	treasure, wealth, valuables
instrukcija	kupka	dijete	blago
封 N2	胸 N2	砂 N2	塩 N2
seal, closing	bosom, breast, chest, heart, feelings	sand	salt
pečat	grudi	pijesak	Sol
賢 N2	腕 N2	兆 N2	床 N2
intelligent, wise, wisdom, cleverness	arm, ability, talent	portent, 10**12, trillion, sign, omen, symptoms	bed, floor, padding, tatami
inteligentan	ručni zglob	bilijuna	krevet
毛 N2	緑 N2	尊 N2	祝 N2
fur, hair, feather, down	green	revered, valuable, precious, noble, exalted	celebrate, congratulate
dlaka	zelena	vrijedan	slaviti
柔 N2	殿 N2	濃 N2	液 N2
tender, weakness, gentleness, softness	Mr., hall, mansion, palace, temple, lord	concentrated, thick, dark, undiluted	fluid, liquid, juice, sap, secretion
ponuda	hram	koncentriraju	tekući

N2	N2	N2	N2
衣	肩	零	幼
garment, clothes, dressing	shoulder	zero, spill, overflow, nothing, cipher	infancy, childhood
odjeća	rame	nula	djetinjstvo
N2	N2	N2	N2
荷	泊	黄	甘
baggage, shoulder-pole load	overnight, put up at, ride at anchor, 3-day stay	yellow	sweet, coax, pamper, be content, sugary
prtljaga	preko noći	žuta boja	slatko
N2	N2	N2	N2
臣	浅	掃	雲
retainer, subject	shallow, superficial, frivolous, wretched, shameful	sweep, brush	cloud
pratilac	plitak	pomesti	oblak
N2	N2	N2	N2
掘	捨	軟	沈
dig, delve, excavate	discard, throw away, abandon, resign, reject	soft	sink, be submerged, subside, be depressed, aloes
kopati	odbaciti	mekan	umivaonik
N2	N2	N2	N2
凍	乳	恋	紅
frozen, congeal, refrigerate	milk, breasts	romance, in love, yearn for, miss, darling	crimson, deep red
zamrznuti	mlijeko	ljubav	Crvena

郊 N2	腰 N2	炭 N2	踊 N2
outskirts, suburbs, rural area	loins, hips, waist, low wainscoting	charcoal, coal	jump, dance, leap, skip
Predgrađe	struk	ugljen	skok
冊 N2	勇 N2	械 N2	菜 N2
tome, counter for books, volume	courage, cheer up, be in high spirits, bravery	contraption, fetter, machine, instrument	vegetable, side dish, greens
meni	Hrabar	instrument	povrće
珍 N2	卵 N2	湖 N2	喫 N2
rare, curious, strange	egg, ovum, spawn, roe	lake	consume, eat, drink, smoke, receive (a blow)
znatiželjan	jaje	jezero	jesti
干 N2	虫 N2	刷 N2	湯 N2
dry, parch	insect, bug, temper	printing, print	hot water, bath, hot spring
suho	insekt	četkanje	Vruća voda
溶 N2	鉱 N2	涙 N2	匹 N2
melt, dissolve, thaw	mineral, ore	tears, sympathy	equal, head, counter for small animals
Otopiti	mineral	suze	jednak

孫 N2 grandchild, descendants unuče	**鋭** N2 pointed, sharpness, edge, weapon, sharp, violent oštrina	**枝** N2 bough, branch, twig, limb grana	**塗** N2 paint, plaster, daub, smear, coating obojen
軒 N2 flats, counter for houses, eaves stanovi	**毒** N2 poison, virus, venom, germ, harm, injury, spite Otrov	**叫** N2 shout, exclaim, yell vikati	**拝** N2 worship, adore, pray to obožavanje
氷 N2 icicle, ice, hail, freeze, congeal ledenica	**乾** N2 drought, dry, dessicate, drink up, heaven, emperor suša	**棒** N2 rod, stick, cane, pole, club, line štap	**祈** N2 pray, wish moliti
拾 N2 pick up, gather, find, go on foot, ten okupiti	**粉** N2 flour, powder, dust puder	**糸** N2 thread nit	**綿** N2 cotton pamuk
汗 N2 sweat, perspire znoj	**銅** N2 copper bakar	**湿** N2 damp, wet, moist smočiti	**瓶** N2 flower pot, bottle, vial, jar, jug, vat, urn boca

N2	N2	N2	N2
咲	召	缶	隻
blossom, bloom	seduce, call, send for, wear, put on, ride in	tin can, container	vessels, counter for ships, fish, birds, arrows
cvijet	zavesti	posuđe	posuđe

N2	N2	N2	N2
脂	蒸	肌	耕
fat, grease, tallow, lard, rosin, gum, tar	steam, heat, sultry, foment, get musty	texture, skin, body, grain	till, plow, cultivate
mast	para	mišić	Plug

N2	N2	N2	N2
鈍	泥	隅	灯
dull, slow, foolish, blunt	mud, mire, adhere to, be attached to	corner, nook	lamp, a light, light, counter for lights
tup	blato	ugao	svjetiljka

N2	N2	N2	N2
辛	磨	麦	姓
spicy, bitter, hot, acrid	grind, polish, scour, improve, brush (teeth)	barley, wheat	surname
začinjeno	samljeti	pšenica	prezime

N2	N2	N2	N2
筒	鼻	粒	詞
cylinder, pipe, tube, gun barrel, sleeve	nose, snout	grains, drop, counter for tiny particles	part of speech, words, poetry
cilindar	nos	žitarica	poezija

N2	N2	N2	N2
胃	**畳**	**机**	**膚**
stomach, paunch, crop, craw	tatami mat, counter for tatami mats, fold	desk, table	skin, body, grain, texture, disposition
trbuh	preklopiti	stol	koža
濯	**塔**	**沸**	**灰**
laundry, wash, pour on, rinse	pagoda, tower, steeple	seethe, boil, ferment, uproar, breed	ashes, puckery juice, cremate
praonica	toranj	Ključanje	pepeo
菓	**帽**	**枯**	**涼**
candy, cakes, fruit	cap, headgear	wither, die, dry up, be seasoned	refreshing, nice and cool
bombon	kapa	uveo	osvježavajući
舟	**貝**	**符**	**憎**
boat, ship	shellfish	token, sign, mark, tally, charm	hate, detest
čamac	školjka	simbol	Mrziti
皿	**肯**	**燥**	**畜**
dish, a helping, plate	agreement, consent, comply with	parch, dry up	livestock, domestic fowl and animals
Jelo	sporazum	suho	stoka

挟 N2 pinch, between prstohvat	**曇** N2 cloudy weather, cloud up oblačno	**滴** N2 drip, drop pad	**伺** N2 pay respects, visit, ask, inquire, question, implore poštovanje
氏 N2 family name, surname, clan prezime	**統** N2 overall, relationship, ruling, governing Cjelokupni	**保** N2 protect, guarantee, keep, preserve, sustain, support zaštititi	**第** N2 No., residence prebivalište
結 N2 tie, bind, contract, join, organize, do up hair ugovor	**派** N2 faction, group, party, clique, sect, school frakcija	**案** N2 plan, suggestion, draft, ponder, fear, proposition prijedlog	**策** N2 scheme, plan, policy, step, means Politika
基 N2 fundamentals, radical (chem), counter for machines osnove	**価** N2 value, price vrijednost	**提** N2 propose, take along, carry in hand predložiti	**挙** N2 raise, plan, project, behavior, actions podići
応 N2 apply, answer, yes, OK, reply, accept primijeniti	**企** N2 undertake, scheme, design, attempt, plan poduzeti	**検** N2 examination, investigate ispit	**沢** N2 swamp Močvara

N1	N1	N1	N1
裁	証	援	施
tailor, judge, decision, cut out (pattern)	evidence, proof, certificate	abet, help, save	alms, apply bandages, administer first-aid
krojač, prilagoditi	potvrda	pomoć	milostinja

N1	N1	N1	N1
井	護	展	態
well, well crib, town, community	safeguard, protect	unfold, expand	attitude, condition, figure, appearance
dobro	Zaštititi	razmotati	stav

N1	N1	N1	N1
鮮	視	条	幹
fresh, vivid, clear, brilliant, Korea	inspection, regard as, see, look at	article, clause, item, stripe, streak	tree trunk
svježe	inspekcija	članak	deblo

N1	N1	N1	N1
独	宮	率	衛
single, alone, spontaneously, Germany	Shinto shrine, constellations, palace, princess	ratio, rate, proportion, %, coefficient, factor	defense, protection
sam	zviježđa	omjer	odbrana

N1	N1	N1	N1
張	監	環	審
lengthen, counter for bows & stringed instruments	oversee, official, govt office, rule, administer	ring, circle, link, wheel	hearing, judge, trial
produljuju	nadgledati	krug	Pregled

義 N1	訴 N1	株 N1	姿 N1
righteousness, justice, morality, honor, loyalty	accusation, sue, complain of pain, appeal to	stocks, stump, shares, stock	figure, form, shape
Pravednost	žaliti se	panj	držanje
閣 N1	衆 N1	評 N1	影 N1
tower, tall building, palace	masses, great numbers, multitude, populace	evaluate, criticism, comment	shadow, silhouette, phantom
toranj	mase	procijeniti	Sjena
松 N1	撃 N1	佐 N1	核 N1
pine tree	beat, attack, defeat, conquer	assistant, help	nucleus, core, kernel
Bor	pobijediti	asistent	nuklearni
整 N1	融 N1	製 N1	票 N1
organize, arranging, tune, tone, meter, key (music)	dissolve, melt	made in..., manufacture	ballot, label, ticket, sign
organizirati	topiti	proizvodnja	glasački listić
渉 N1	響 N1	推 N1	請 N1
ford, ferry, port	echo, also N5116, sound, resound, ring, vibrate	conjecture, infer, guess, suppose, support	solicit, invite, ask
trajekt	jeka	pretpostavka	Molim

N1	N1	N1	N1
器 utensil, vessel, receptacle, implement, instrument alatka	士 gentleman, samurai gospodin	討 chastise, attack, defeat, destroy, conquer kazniti	攻 aggression, attack napad
崎 promontory, cape, spit rt	督 coach, command, urge, lead, supervise trener	授 impart, instruct, grant, confer Grant	催 sponsor, hold (a meeting), give (a dinner) sponzor
及 reach out, exert, exercise, cause vršiti	憲 constitution, law ustav	摘 pinch, pick, pluck, trim, clip, summarize Odabrati	系 lineage, system loza
批 criticism, strike kritika	郎 son, counter for sons sin	健 healthy, health, strength, persistence Zdrav	盟 alliance, oath savez
従 accompany, obey, submit to, comply, follow pratiti	修 discipline, conduct oneself well, study, master disciplina	隊 regiment, party, company, squad puk	織 weave, fabric Tkati

拡 N1	故 N1	振 N1	弁 N1
broaden, extend, expand, enlarge	happenstance, especially	shake, wave, wag, swing	valve, petal, braid, speech, dialect, discrimination
proširiti	slučajnost	tresti	ventil
就 N1	異 N1	献 N1	厳 N1
concerning, settle, take position, depart	uncommon, queerness, strangeness, wonderful	offering, counter for drinks, present, offer	stern, strictness, severity, rigidity
o	rijedak	ponuda	krma
維 N1	浜 N1	遺 N1	塁 N1
fiber, tie, rope	seacoast, beach, seashore	bequeath, leave behind, reserve	bases, fort, rampart, walls, base(ball)
vlakno	plaža	zavještati	baze
邦 N1	素 N1	遣 N1	抗 N1
home country, country, Japan	elementary, principle, naked, uncovered	despatch, send, give, donate, do, undertake	confront, resist, defy, oppose
zemlja	osnovni	otpremanje	suočiti
模 N1	雄 N1	益 N1	緊 N1
imitation, copy, mock	masculine, male, hero, leader, superiority	benefit, gain, profit, advantage	tense, solid, hard, reliable, tight
imitacija	muški	blagotvoran	tijesan

標 (N1)	宣 (N1)	昭 (N1)	廃 (N1)
signpost, seal, mark, stamp, imprint	proclaim, say, announce	shining, bright	abolish, obsolete, cessation, discarding, abandon
pečat	proglasiti	svijetao	ukinuti

伊 (N1)	江 (N1)	僚 (N1)	吉 (N1)
Italy, that one	creek, inlet, bay	colleague, official, companion	good luck, joy, congratulations
Italija	potok	Suradnik	Čestitamo

皇 (N1)	臨 (N1)	踏 (N1)	壊 (N1)
emperor	look to, face, meet, confront, attend, call on	step, trample, carry through, appraise	demolition, break, destroy
Car	lice	zgaziti	rušenje

債 (N1)	興 (N1)	源 (N1)	儀 (N1)
bond, loan, debt	entertain, revive, retrieve, interest, pleasure	source, origin	ceremony, rule, affair, case, a matter
dug	zabaviti	izvor	ceremonija

創 (N1)	障 (N1)	継 (N1)	筋 (N1)
genesis, wound, injury, hurt, start, originate	hinder, hurt, harm	inherit, succeed, patch, graft (tree)	muscle, sinew, tendon, fiber, plot, plan, descent
geneza	ometati	naslijediti	mišić

闘 N1	葬 N1	避 N1	司 N1
fight, war	interment, bury, shelve	evade, avoid, avert, ward off, shirk, shun	director, official, govt office, rule, administer
borba	sahrana	Izbjegavajte	direktor
康 N1	善 N1	逮 N1	迫 N1
ease, peace	virtuous, good, goodness	apprehend, chase	urge, force, imminent, spur on
ublažiti	dobro	shvatiti	sila
惑 N1	崩 N1	紀 N1	聴 N1
beguile, delusion, perplexity	crumble, die, demolish, level	chronicle, account, narrative, history, annals	listen, headstrong, naughty, careful inquiry
obmana	mrviti	kronika	slušati
脱 N1	級 N1	博 N1	締 N1
undress, removing, escape from, get rid of	class, rank, grade	Dr., command, esteem, win acclaim, Ph.D.,	tighten, tie, shut, lock, fasten
svući se	nivo	poštovanje	zategnuti
救 N1	執 N1	房 N1	撤 N1
salvation, save, help, rescue, reclaim	tenacious, take hold, grasp, take to heart	tassel, tuft, fringe, bunch, lock (hair)	remove, withdraw, disarm, dismantle, reject, exclude
uštedjeti	uporan	resa	povući

N1 削 plane, sharpen, whittle, pare izoštriti	**N1** 密 secrecy, density (pop), minuteness, carefulness tajnost	**N1** 措 set aside, give up, suspend, discontinue, lay aside obustaviti	**N1** 志 intention, plan, resolve, aspire, motive, hopes namjera
N1 載 ride, board, get on, place, spread, 10**44 vožnja	**N1** 陣 camp, battle array, ranks, position kamp	**N1** 我 ego, I, selfish, our, oneself ja	**N1** 為 do, change, make, benefit korist
N1 抑 repress, well, now, in the first place, push potisnuti	**N1** 幕 curtain, bunting, act of play zavjesa	**N1** 染 dye, color, paint, stain, print boja	**N1** 奈 Nara, what? što
N1 傷 wound, hurt, injure, impair, pain, injury, cut povrijediti	**N1** 択 choose, select, elect, prefer izabrati	**N1** 秀 excel, excellence, beauty, surpass izvrsnost	**N1** 徴 indications, sign, omen, symptom, collect, seek indikacije
N1 弾 bullet, twang, flip, snap metak	**N1** 償 reparation, make up for, recompense, redeem reparacija	**N1** 功 achievement, merits, success, honor, credit dostignuće	**N1** 拠 foothold, based on, follow, therefore uporište

秘 N1	拒 N1	刑 N1	塚 N1
secret, conceal	repel, refuse, reject, decline	punish, penalty, sentence, punishment	hillock, mound
tajna	Odbiti	kazna	nasip
致 N1	繰 N1	尾 N1	描 N1
doth, do, send, forward, cause, exert, incur, engage	winding, reel, spin, turn (pages), look up, refer to	tail, end, counter for fish, lower slope of mountain	sketch, compose, write, draw, paint
naprijed	špula	rep	Skica
鈴 N1	盤 N1	項 N1	喪 N1
small bell, buzzer	tray, shallow bowl, platter, tub, board	paragraph, nape of neck, clause, item	miss, mourning
zvono	ladica	stav	žalost
伴 N1	養 N1	懸 N1	街 N1
consort, accompany, bring with, companion	foster, bring up, rear, develop, nurture	suspend, hang, 10%, install, depend, consult	boulevard, street, town
drug	gajiti	obustaviti	ulica
契 N1	掲 N1	躍 N1	棄 N1
pledge, promise, vow	put up (a notice), put up, hoist, display	leap, dance, skip	abandon, throw away, discard, resign, reject
zalog	dizalica	skok	napušten

邸 N1	縮 N1	還 N1	属 N1
residence, mansion	shrink, contract, shrivel, wrinkle, reduce	send back, return	belong, genus, subordinate official, affiliated
prebivalište	Se smanjiti	povratak	pripadaju
慮 N1	枠 N1	恵 N1	露 N1
prudence, thought, concern, consider, deliberate	frame, framework, spindle, spool	favor, blessing, grace, kindness	dew, tears, expose, Russia
smatrati	okvir	milost	rosa
節 N1	需 N1	射 N1	購 N1
, clause, stanza, honor, joint, knuckle, knob, knot	demand, request, need	shoot, shine into, onto, archery	subscription, buy
razdoblje	zahtijevajte	Pucati	kupiti
揮 N1	充 N1	貢 N1	鹿 N1
brandish, wave, wag, swing, shake	allot, fill	tribute, support, finance	deer
Val	dodijeliti	danak	jelen
却 N1	端 N1	賃 N1	獲 N1
instead, on the contrary, rather	edge, origin, end, point, border, verge, cape	fare, fee, hire, rent, wages, charge	seize, get, find, earn, acquire, can, may, able to
ali	kraj	najam	dobit

郡 N1	併 N1	徹 N1	貴 N1
county, district	join, get together, unite, collective	penetrate, clear, pierce, strike home	precious, value, prize, esteem, honor
okrug	pridružiti	prodrijeti	dragocjen
衝 N1	焦 N1	奪 N1	災 N1
collide, brunt, highway, opposition (astronomy)	char, hurry, impatient, irritate, burn, scorch	rob, take by force, snatch away, dispossess, plunder	disaster, calamity, woe, curse, evil
sudaraju	žuriti	opljačkati	katastrofa
浦 N1	析 N1	譲 N1	称 N1
bay, creek, inlet, gulf, beach, seacoast	chop, divide, tear, analyze	defer, turnover, transfer, convey	appellation, praise, admire, name, title, fame
zaljev	nasjeckati	promet	imenovanje
納 N1	樹 N1	挑 N1	誘 N1
settlement, obtain, reap, pay, supply, store	timber trees, wood	challenge, contend for, make love to	entice, lead, tempt, invite, ask, call for
naselje	drvo	izazov	primamiti
紛 N1	至 N1	宗 N1	促 N1
distract, be mistaken for, go astray, divert	climax, arrive, proceed, reach, attain, result in	religion, sect, denomination, main point, origin	stimulate, urge, press, demand, incite
odvratiti	vrhunac	religija	stimulirati

N1	N1	N1	N1
慎	控	智	握
humility, be careful, discrete, prudent	withdraw, draw in, hold back, refrain from	wisdom, intellect, reason	grip, hold, mould sushi, bribe
poniznost	povući	mudrost	zahvat

N1	N1	N1	N1
宙	俊	銭	渋
mid-air, air, space, sky, memorization	sagacious, genius, excellence	coin, .01 yen, money	astringent, hesitate, reluctant, have diarrhea
svemir	mudar	novac	oklijevati

N1	N1	N1	N1
銃	操	携	診
gun, arms	maneuver, manipulate, operate, steer, chastity	portable, carry (in hand), armed with, bring along	checkup, seeing, diagnose, examine
pištolj	manipulirati	prijenos	pregled

N1	N1	N1	N1
託	撮	誕	侵
consign, requesting, entrusting with, pretend, hint	snapshot, take pictures	nativity, be born, declension, lie, be arbitrary	encroach, invade, raid, trespass, violate
poslati	snimak	Mala Gospojina	povrijediti

N1	N1	N1	N1
括	謝	駆	透
fasten, tie up, arrest, constrict	apologize, thank, refuse	drive, run, gallop, advance, inspire, impel	transparent, permeate, filter, penetrate
pričvrstiti	ispričavati	voziti	transparentan

津 N1	壁 N1	稲 N1	仮 N1
haven, port, harbor, ferry	wall, lining (stomach), fence	rice plant	sham, temporary, interim, assumed (name), informal
luka	zid	biljka riže	privremen

裂 N1	敏 N1	是 N1	排 N1
split, rend, tear	cleverness, agile, alert	just so, this, right, justice	repudiate, exclude, expel, reject
pukotina	pamet	pravda	odbaciti

裕 N1	堅 N1	訳 N1	芝 N1
abundant, rich, fertile	strict, hard, solid, tough, tight, reliable	translate, reason, circumstance, case	turf, lawn
obilan	strog	Prevedi	travnjak

綱 N1	典 N1	賀 N1	扱 N1
hawser, class (genus), rope, cord, cable	code, ceremony, law, rule	congratulations, joy	handle, entertain, thresh, strip
uže	Kodirati	Čestitati	ručica

顧 N1	弘 N1	看 N1	訟 N1
look back, review, examine oneself, turn around	vast, broad, wide	watch over, see	sue, accuse
pregled	širok	vidjeti	optužiti

N1	N1	N1	N1
戒 commandment zapovijed	祉 welfare, happiness blagostanje	誉 reputation, praise, honor, glory ugled	歓 delight, joy zadovoljstvo
奏 play music, speak to a ruler, complete igra	勧 persuade, recommend, advise, encourage, offer uvjeriti	騒 boisterous, make noise, clamor, disturb, excite buka	閥 clique, lineage, pedigree, faction, clan klika
甲 armor, high (voice), A grade, first class, former oklop	縄 straw rope, cord vrpca	郷 home town, village, native place, district selo	揺 swing, shake, sway, rock, tremble, vibrate ljuljati
免 excuse, dismissal izgovor	既 previously, already, long ago prethodno	薦 recommend, mat, advise, encourage, offer Preporuči	隣 neighboring susjedan
華 splendor, flower, petal, shine, luster, ostentatious sjaj	範 pattern, example, model uzorak	隠 conceal, hide, cover prikriti	徳 benevolence, virtue, goodness, commanding respect dobrota

哲 N1	杉 N1	釈 N1	己 N1
philosophy, clear	cedar, cryptomeria	explanation	self, snake, serpent
filozofija	kedar	obrazloženje	zmija
妥 N1	威 N1	豪 N1	熊 N1
gentle, peace, depravity	intimidate, dignity, majesty, menace, threaten	overpowering, great, powerful, excelling, Australia	bear
nježan	Prestiž	neodoljiv	Snositi
滞 N1	微 N1	隆 N1	症 N1
stagnate, be delayed, overdue, arrears	delicate, minuteness, insignificance	hump, high, noble, prosperity	symptoms, illness
Stagnacija	delikatan	grba	simptomi
暫 N1	忠 N1	倉 N1	彦 N1
temporarily, a while, moment, long time	loyalty, fidelity, faithfulness	godown, warehouse, storehouse, cellar, treasury	lad, boy (ancient)
privremeno	Odan	skladište	dječak
肝 N1	喚 N1	沿 N1	妙 N1
liver, pluck, nerve, chutzpah	yell, cry, scream	run alongside, follow along, run along, lie along	exquisite, strange, queer, mystery, miracle
jetra	plakati	uz	predivan

N1 唱	N1 阿	N1 索	N1 誠
chant, recite, call upon, yell	Africa, flatter, fawn upon, corner, nook, recess	cord, rope	sincerity, admonish, warn, prohibit, truth
pjevati	Afrika	uže	iskrenost
N1 襲	N1 懇	N1 俳	N1 柄
attack, advance on, succeed to, pile, heap	sociable, kind, courteous, hospitable, cordial	haiku, actor	design, pattern, build, nature, handle, crank
napad	društven	glumac	oblikovati
N1 驚	N1 麻	N1 李	N1 浩
wonder, be surprised, frightened, amazed	hemp, flax	plum	wide expanse, abundance, vigorous
čudo	konoplja	šljiva	obilje
N1 剤	N1 瀬	N1 趣	N1 陥
dose, medicine, drug	rapids, current, torrent, shallows, shoal	gist, proceed to, tend, become	collapse, fall into, cave in, fall (castle)
lijek	Trenutno	postati	kolaps
N1 斎	N1 貫	N1 仙	N1 慰
purification, Buddhist food, room, worship, avoid	pierce, 8 1, 3lbs, penetrate, brace	hermit, wizard, cent	consolation, amusement, seduce, cheer, console
pročišćavanje	probušiti	pustinjak	udobnost

序 N1	兼 N1	聖 N1	旨 N1
preface, beginning, order, precedence, occasion	concurrently, and	holy, saint, sage, master, priest	delicious, relish, show a liking for, purport, will
predgovor	istovremeno	svet	ukusno
即 N1	柳 N1	舎 N1	偽 N1
instant, namely, as is, conform, agree, adapt	willow	cottage, inn, hut, house, mansion	falsehood, lie, deceive, pretend, counterfeit
trenutak	vrba	kućica	laž
較 N1	覇 N1	詳 N1	抵 N1
contrast, compare	hegemony, supremacy, leadership, champion	detailed, full, minute, accurate, well-informed	resist, reach, touch
Usporedite	hegemonija	detaljan	odoljeti
脅 N1	茂 N1	犠 N1	旗 N1
threaten, coerce	overgrown, grow thick, be luxuriant	sacrifice	national flag, banner, standard
Ugroziti	obrastao	žrtva	zastava
距 N1	雅 N1	飾 N1	網 N1
long-distance	gracious, elegant, graceful, refined	decorate, ornament, adorn, embellish	netting, network
udaljenost	elegantan	Ukrasiti	mreža

N1	N1	N1	N1
竜 dragon, imperial zmaj	詩 poem, poetry poezija	繁 luxuriant, thick, overgrown, frequency, complexity komplicirano	翼 wing, plane, flank krilo
潟 lagoon laguna	敵 enemy, foe, opponent neprijatelj	魅 fascination, charm, bewitch Draž	嫌 dislike, detest, hate sumnjiv
斉 adjusted, alike, equal, similar variety of prilagođen	敷 spread, pave, sit, promulgate širenje	擁 hug, embrace, possess, protect, lead zagrliti	圏 sphere, circle, radius, range sfera
酸 acid, bitterness, sour, tart kiselina	罰 penalty, punishment Kazniti	滅 destroy, ruin, overthrow, perish uništiti	礎 cornerstone, foundation stone temelj
腐 rot, decay, sour Istrunuti	潮 tide, salt water, opportunity plima	梅 plum šljiva	尽 exhaust, use up, run out of, befriend, serve Ispušni

僕 N1	桜 N1	滑 N1	孤 N1
me, I (male)	cherry	slippery, slide, slip, flunk	orphan, alone
mi	trešnja	klizav	siroče
炎 N1	賠 N1	句 N1	鋼 N1
inflammation, flame, blaze	compensation, indemnify	phrase, clause, sentence, passage, paragraph	steel
upala	kompenzacija	fraza	željezo
頑 N1	鎖 N1	彩 N1	摩 N1
stubborn, foolish, firmly	chain, irons, connection	coloring, paint, makeup	chafe, rub, polish, grind, scrape
tvrdoglav	lanac	bojanje	polirati
励 N1	縦 N1	輝 N1	蓄 N1
encourage, be diligent, inspire	vertical, length, height, self-indulgent, wayward	radiance, shine, sparkle, gleam, twinkle	amass, keeping a concubine, phonograph
ohrabriti	vertikala	sjajan	fonograf
軸 N1	巡 N1	稼 N1	瞬 N1
axis, pivot, stem, stalk, counter for book scrolls	patrol, go around, circumference	earnings, work, earn money	wink, blink, twinkle
os	patrola	zarada	mig

砲 N1 cannon, gun puška	**噴** N1 erupt, spout, emit, flush out sprej
誇 N1 boast, be proud, pride, triumphantly hvalisati se	**祥** N1 auspicious, happiness, good omen Povoljan
牲 N1 animal sacrifice, offering Žrtva	**秩** N1 regularity, salary, order plaća
帝 N1 sovereign, the emperor, god, creator car	**宏** N1 wide, large širok
唆 N1 tempt, seduce, instigate, promote iskušavate	**阻** N1 thwart, separate from, prevent, obstruct, deter spriječiti
泰 N1 peaceful, calm, peace, easy, Thailand mirno	**賄** N1 bribe, board, supply, finance mito
撲 N1 slap, strike, hit, beat, tell, speak šamar	**堀** N1 ditch, moat, canal jarak
菊 N1 chrysanthemum hrizantema	**絞** N1 strangle, constrict, wring daviti
縁 N1 affinity, relation, connection, edge, border sklonost	**唯** N1 solely, only, merely, simply samo
膨 N1 swell, get fat, thick naduti	**矢** N1 dart, arrow strijelica

N1	N1	N1	N1
耐 -proof, enduring trajan	塾 cram school, private school privatna škola	漏 leak, escape, time curenje	慶 jubilation, congratulate, rejoice, be happy Slaviti
猛 fierce, rave, rush, become furious, wildness bijesan	芳 perfume, balmy, flavorable, fragrant parfem	懲 penal, chastise, punish, discipline kazneni	剣 sabre, sword, blade, clock hand Mač
彰 patent, clear patent	棋 chess piece, Japanese chess, shogi šah	丁 street, ward, town ulica	恒 constancy, always Konstantno
揚 hoist, fry in deep fat dizalica	冒 risk, face, defy, dare, damage, assume (a name) Rizik	之 of, this ovaj	倫 ethics, companion drug
陳 exhibit, state, relate, explain izložak	憶 recollection, think, remember Podsjetiti	梨 pear tree kruška	仁 humanity, virtue, benevolence, charity, man, kernel dobronamjernost

N1	N1	N1	N1
克	岳	概	拘
overcome, kindly, skillfully	point, peak, mountain	outline, condition, approximation, generally	arrest, seize, concerned, adhere to, despite
savladati	točka	obris	uhapsiti
墓	**黙**	**須**	**偏**
grave, tomb	silence, become silent, stop speaking, leave as is	ought, by all means, necessarily	partial, side, left-side radical, inclining, biased
grob	tišina	obavezno	parcijalan
雰	**遇**	**諮**	**狭**
atmosphere, fog	interview, treat, entertain, receive, deal with	consult with	cramped, narrow, contract, tight
atmosfera	intervju	Savjetovati	suziti
卓	**亀**	**糧**	**簿**
eminent, table, desk, high	tortoise, turtle	provisions, food, bread	register, record book
eminentan	kornjača	žitarica	Registar
炉	**牧**	**殊**	**殖**
hearth, furnace, kiln, reactor	breed, care for, shepherd, feed, pasture	particularly, especially, exceptionally	augment, increase, multiply, raise
peć	vrsta	poseban	povećati

艦 N1 warship ratni brod	**輩** N1 comrade, fellow, people, companions drug	**穴** N1 hole, aperture, slit, cave, den rupa	**奇** N1 strange, strangeness, curiosity neparan
慢 N1 ridicule, laziness ismijavati	**鶴** N1 crane, stork dizalica	**謀** N1 conspire, cheat, impose on, plan, devise, scheme kovati zavjeru	**暖** N1 warmth toplina
昌 N1 prosperous, bright, clear uspješan	**拍** N1 clap, beat (music) pljeskati	**朗** N1 melodious, clear, bright, serene, cheerful melodičan	**寛** N1 tolerant, leniency, generosity, relax, feel at home tolerantan
覆 N1 capsize, cover, shade, mantle, be ruined pokriti	**胞** N1 placenta, sac, sheath korice	**泣** N1 cry, weep, moan plakati	**隔** N1 isolate, alternate, distance, separate, gulf izolat
浄 N1 clean, purify, cleanse, exorcise, Manchu Dynasty čist	**没** N1 drown, sink, hide, fall into, disappear, die utopiti	**暇** N1 spare time, rest, leisure, time, leave of absence slobodno vrijeme	**肺** N1 lungs pluća

貞 N1 upright, chastity, constancy, righteousness uspravan	**靖** N1 peaceful mirno	**鑑** N1 specimen, take warning from, learn from primjerak	**飼** N1 domesticate, raise, keep, feed udomaćiti
陰 N1 shade, yin, negative, sex organs, secret, shadow hlad	**銘** N1 inscription, signature (of artisan) natpis	**随** N1 follow, though, notwithstanding slijediti	**烈** N1 ardent, violent, vehement, furious, severe, extreme žarki
尋 N1 inquire, fathom, look for raspitati	**稿** N1 draft, copy, manuscript, straw Nacrt	**丹** N1 rust-colored, red, red lead, pills Crvena	**啓** N1 disclose, open, say otkriti
也 N1 to be (classical) I također	**丘** N1 hill, knoll brdo	**壤** N1 lot, earth, soil tlo	**漫** N1 cartoon, involuntarily, in spite of oneself crtani film
玄 N1 mysterious, occultness misteriozan	**粘** N1 sticky, glutinous, greasy, persevere štap	**悟** N1 enlightenment, perceive, discern, realize prosvjećivanje	**舗** N1 shop, store dućan

妊 N1	熟 N1	旭 N1	恩 N1
pregnancy	mellow, ripen, mature, acquire skill	rising sun, morning sun	grace, kindness, goodness, favor, mercy
Trudnoća	pripit	Sunce	ljubaznost
騰 N1	往 N1	豆 N1	遂 N1
inflation, advancing, going	journey, chase away, let go, going, travel	beans, pea, midget	consummate, accomplish, attain, commit (suicide)
inflacija	putovanje	grah	besprijekoran
狂 N1	岐 N1	陛 N1	緯 N1
lunatic, insane, crazy, confuse	branch off, fork in road, scene, arena, theater	highness, steps (of throne)	horizontal, woof, left & right, latitude
luđak	scena	visost	vodoravan
培 N1	衰 N1	艇 N1	屈 N1
cultivate, foster	decline, wane, weaken	rowboat, small boat	yield, bend, flinch, submit
njegovati	odbiti	Čamac	zavoj
径 N1	淡 N1	抽 N1	披 N1
diameter, path, method	thin, faint, pale, fleeting	pluck, pull, extract, excel	expose, open
staza	blijed	osmjeliti	ekspoze

廷 N1	錦 N1	准 N1	暑 N1
courts, imperial court, government office	brocade, fine dress, honors	quasi-, semi-, associate	sultry, hot, summer heat
sudovi	Brokat	suradnik	toplina
磯 N1	奨 N1	浸 N1	剰 N1
seashore, beach	exhort, urge, encourage	immersed, soak, dip, steep, moisten, wet, dunk	surplus, besides
morska obala	potaknuti	uronjen	višak
胆 N1	繊 N1	駒 N1	虚 N1
gall bladder, courage, pluck, nerve	slender, fine, thin kimono	pony, horse, colt	void, emptiness, unpreparedness, crack, fissure
hrabrost	vitak	Ždrijebe	praznina
霊 N1	帳 N1	悔 N1	諭 N1
spirits, soul	notebook, account book, album	repent, regret	rebuke, admonish, charge, warn, persuade
duhovi	bilježnica	žaljenje	ukor
惨 N1	虐 N1	翻 N1	墜 N1
wretched, disaster, cruelty, harsh	tyrannize, oppress	flip, turn over, wave, flutter, change (mind)	crash, fall (down)
grozan	tlače	skretanje	pad

沼 N1 marsh, lake, bog, swamp, pond močvara	**据** N1 set, lay a foundation, install, equip, squat down prema	**肥** N1 fertilizer, get fat, fertile, manure, pamper gnojivo	**徐** N1 gradually, slowly, deliberately, gently postepeno
糖 N1 sugar šećer	**搭** N1 board, load (a vehicle), ride vožnja	**盾** N1 shield, escutcheon, pretext štit	**脈** N1 vein, pulse, hope puls
滝 N1 waterfall, rapids, cascade slap	**軌** N1 rut, wheel, track, model, way of doing navika	**俵** N1 bag, bale, sack, counter for bags torba	**妨** N1 disturb, prevent, hamper, obstruct poremetiti
擦 N1 grate, rub, scratch, scrape, chafe, scour trljati	**鯨** N1 whale kit	**荘** N1 villa, inn, cottage, feudal manor gostionica	**諾** N1 consent, assent, agreement pristanak
雷 N1 thunder, lightening bolt grmljavina	**漂** N1 drift, float (on liquid) zanošenje	**懐** N1 pocket, feelings, heart, yearn, miss someone osjećaji	**勘** N1 intuition, perception intuicija

栽 N1	拐 N1	駄 N1	添 N1
plantation, planting	kidnap, falsify	burdensome, pack horse, horse load, send by horse	annexed, accompany, marry, suit, meet
sjetva	oteti	tegoban	pratiti
冠 N1	斜 N1	鏡 N1	聡 N1
crown, best, peerless	diagonal, slanting, oblique	mirror, speculum, barrel-head	wise, fast learner
kruna	dijagonala	ogledalo	mudar
浪 N1	亜 N1	覧 N1	詐 N1
wandering, waves, billows	Asia, rank next, come after, -ous	perusal, see	lie, falsehood, deceive, pretend
val	Azija	lektira	laž
壇 N1	勲 N1	魔 N1	酬 N1
podium, stage, rostrum, terrace	meritorious deed, merit	witch, demon, evil spirit	repay, reward, retribution
podijum	zasluga	vještica	vratiti
紫 N1	曙 N1	紋 N1	卸 N1
purple, violet	dawn, daybreak	family crest, figures	wholesale
purpurna boja	Zora	Uzorak	veleprodaja

N1	N1	N1	N1
奮	欄	逸	涯
stirred up, be invigorated, flourish	column, handrail, blank, space	deviate, idleness, leisure, miss the mark, evade	horizon, shore
procvjetati	stupac	odstupati	horizont
拓	眼	獄	尚
clear (the land), open, break up (land)	eyeball	prison, jail	esteem, furthermore, still, yet
nastavak	oko	zatvor	poštovanje
彫	穏	顕	巧
carve, engrave, chisel	calm, quiet, moderation	appear, existing	adroit, skilled, ingenuity
rezbariti	smiriti	pojaviti	genijalnost
矛	垣	欺	萩
halberd, arms, festival float	hedge, fence, wall	deceit, cheat, delude	bush clover
helebarda	zaštititi	obmana	djetelina grma
粛	栗	愚	遭
solemn, quietly, softly	chestnut	foolish, folly, absurdity, stupid	encounter, meet, party, association, interview
svečan	kesten	glup	susret

架 (N1)	鬼 (N1)	庶 (N1)	稚 (N1)
erect, frame, mount, support, shelf, construct	ghost, devil	commoner, all, bastard	immature, young
okvir	duh	prost	naivan

滋 (N1)	幻 (N1)	煮 (N1)	姫 (N1)
nourishing, more & more, be luxuriant	phantasm, vision, dream, illusion, apparition	boil, cook	princess
Hraniti	fantazma	kuhati	princeza

誓 (N1)	把 (N1)	践 (N1)	呈 (N1)
vow, swear, pledge	grasp, faggot, bunch, counter for bundles	tread, step on, trample, practice, carry through	display, offer, present, send, exhibit
psovati	shvatiti	Praksa	prikaz

疎 (N1)	仰 (N1)	剛 (N1)	疾 (N1)
alienate, rough, neglect, shun, sparse	face-up, look up, depend, seek, respect, rever	sturdy, strength	rapidly
otuđiti	tražiti	čvrst	brzo

征 (N1)	砕 (N1)	嫁 (N1)	謙 (N1)
subjugate, attack the rebellious, collect taxes	smash, break, crush, familiar, popular	marry into, bride	self-effacing, humble oneself, condescend
pokoriti	razbiti	nevjesta	skroman

后 N1 empress, queen, after, behind, back, later carica	**嘆** N1 sigh, lament, moan, grieve uzdah	**菌** N1 germ, fungus, bacteria bakterija	**鎌** N1 sickle, scythe, trick srp
巣 N1 nest, rookery, hive, cobweb, den gnijezdo	**頻** N1 repeatedly, recur frekvencija	**琴** N1 harp, koto harfa	**班** N1 squad, corps, unit, group odjeljenje
棚 N1 shelf, ledge, rack, mount, mantle, trellis polica	**潔** N1 undefiled, pure, clean, righteous, gallant neokaljan	**酷** N1 cruel, severe, atrocious, unjust okrutan	**宰** N1 superintend, manager, rule rukovoditi
廊 N1 corridor, hall, tower hodnik	**寂** N1 loneliness, quietly, mellow, mature usamljen	**辰** N1 sign of the dragon, 7-9AM zmaj	**霞** N1 be hazy, grow dim, blurred zamagljen
伏 N1 prostrated, bend down, bow, cover, lay (pipes) ničice	**碁** N1 Go Ići	**俗** N1 vulgar, customs, manners, worldliness Vulgaran	**漠** N1 vague, obscure, desert, wide pustinja

邪 N1	**晶** N1	**墨** N1	**鎮** N1
wicked, injustice, wrong	sparkle, clear, crystal	black ink, India ink, ink stick, Mexico	tranquilize, ancient peace-preservation centers
zlo	kristal	tinta	stišati
洞 N1	**履** N1	**劣** N1	**那** N1
den, cave, excavation	footgear, shoes, boots, put on (the feet	inferiority, be inferior to, be worse	what?
špilja	cipela	inferioran	što?
殴 N1	**娠** N1	**奉** N1	**憂** N1
assault, hit, beat, thrash	with child, pregnancy	observance, offer, present, dedicate	melancholy, grieve, lament, be anxious, sad
napad	trudna	propis	sjeta
朴 N1	**亭** N1	**淳** N1	**怪** N1
crude, simple, plain, docile	pavilion, restaurant, mansion, arbor, cottage	pure	suspicious, mystery, apparition
Sirovi	paviljon	čist	sumnjiv
鳩 N1	**酔** N1	**惜** N1	**穫** N1
pigeon, dove	drunk, feel sick, poisoned, elated, spellbound	pity, be sparing of, frugal, stingy, regret	harvest, reap
Golub	pijan	Šteta	žetva

Kanji	Meaning	Croatian
佳 (N1)	excellent, beautiful, good, pleasing, skilled	izvrstan
潤 (N1)	wet, be watered, profit by, receive benefits	ovlažiti
悼 (N1)	lament, grieve over	naricati
乏 (N1)	destitution, scarce, limited	bijeda
該 (N1)	above-stated, the said, that specific	specifično
赴 (N1)	proceed, get, become, tend	postupiti
桑 (N1)	mulberry	dud
桂 (N1)	Japanese Judas-tree, cinnamon tree	cimet stablo
髄 (N1)	marrow, pith	Srž
虎 (N1)	tiger, drunkard	tigar
盆 (N1)	basin, lantern festival, tray	bazen
晋 (N1)	advance	unaprijed
穂 (N1)	ear, ear (grain), head, crest (wave)	uho
壮 (N1)	robust, manhood, prosperity	jak
堤 (N1)	dike, bank, embankment	nasip
飢 (N1)	hungry, starve	gladan
傍 (N1)	bystander, side, besides, while, nearby, 3rd person	posmatrač
疫 (N1)	epidemic	epidemija
累 (N1)	accumulate, involvement, trouble, tie up	akumulirati
痴 (N1)	stupid, foolish	Idiot

N1	N1	N1	N1
搬 conveyor, carry, transport pomicati	晃 clear čisto	癒 healing, cure, quench (thirst), wreak liječenje	寸 measurement, foot, 10 mjerenje
郭 enclosure, quarters, fortification prilog	尿 urine urin	凶 villain, evil, bad luck, disaster zlikovac	吐 spit, vomit, belch, confess, tell (lies) pljunuti
宴 banquet, feast, party banket	鷹 hawk orao	賓 V.I.P., guest gost	虜 captive, barbarian, low epithet for the enemy zarobljenik
陶 pottery, porcelain posuđe	鐘 bell, gong, chimes zvono	憾 remorse, regret, be sorry žaljenje	猪 boar svinja
紘 large veliki	磁 magnet, porcelain magnetski	弥 all the more, increasingly sve	昆 descendants, elder brother, insect potomci

粗 N1	訂 N1	芽 N1	庄 N1
coarse, rough, rugged	revise, correct, decide	bud, sprout, spear, germ	level
grub	revidirati	pupoljak	nivo
傘 N1	敦 N1	騎 N1	寧 N1
umbrella	industry, kindliness	equestrian, riding on horses	rather, preferably
kišobran	industrija	konjanički	radije
循 N1	忍 N1	怠 N1	如 N1
sequential, fellow	endure, bear, put up with, conceal, secrete	neglect, laziness	likeness, like, such as, as if, better, best, equal
sekvencijalno	podnijeti	zanemariti	sličnost
寮 N1	祐 N1	鵬 N1	鉛 N1
dormitory, hostel, villa, tea pavillion	help	phoenix	lead
spavaonica	Pomozite	Feniks	voditi
珠 N1	苗 N1	獣 N1	哀 N1
pearl, gem, jewel	seedling, sapling, shoot	animal, beast	pathetic, grief, sorrow, pathos, pity, sympathize
biser	sjemenjača	životinja	patetičan

跳 N1	匠 N1	垂 N1	蛇 N1
hop, leap up, spring, jerk, prance, buck, splash	artisan, workman, carpenter	droop, suspend, hang, slouch	snake, serpent, hard drinker
skok	obrtnik	klonuti	zmija
澄 N1	縫 N1	僧 N1	眺 N1
lucidity, be clear, clear, clarify, settle, strain	sew, stitch, embroider	Buddhist priest, monk	stare, watch, look at, see, scrutinize
Čisto	sašiti	redovnik	buljiti
亘 N1	呉 N1	凡 N1	憩 N1
span, request	give, do something for	mediocre	recess, rest, relax, repose
pedalj	dati	osrednji	udubljenje
媛 N1	溝 N1	恭 N1	刈 N1
beautiful woman, princess	gutter, ditch, sewer, drain, 10**32	respect, reverent	reap, cut, clip, trim, prune
princeza	žlijeb	poštovanje	žeti
睡 N1	錯 N1	伯 N1	笹 N1
drowsy, sleep, die	confused, mix, be in disorder	chief, count, earl, uncle, Brazil	bamboo grass
mamuran	zbunjen	glavni	bambusova trava

穀 N1	陵 N1	霧 N1	魂 N1
cereals, grain	mausoleum, imperial tomb	fog, mist	soul, spirit
žitarice	mauzolej	magla	duša
弊 N1	妃 N1	舶 N1	餓 N1
abuse, evil, vice, breakage	queen, princess	liner, ship	starve, hungry, thirst
zlostavljanje	kraljica	brod	gladan
窮 N1	掌 N1	麗 N1	綾 N1
hard up, destitute, suffer, perplexed, cornered	manipulate, rule, administer, conduct, palm of hand	lovely, companion	design, figured cloth, twill
patiti	manipulirati	lijep	oblikovati
臭 N1	悦 N1	刃 N1	縛 N1
stinking, ill-smelling, suspicious looking	ecstasy, joy, rapture	blade, sword, edge	truss, arrest, bind, tie, restrain
smrdljiv	Zadovoljan	oštrica	krovište
暦 N1	宜 N1	盲 N1	粋 N1
calendar, almanac	best regards, good	blind, blind man, ignoramus	chic, style, purity, essence, pith, cream, elite
kalendar	Lijepi Pozdrav	zaslijepiti	šik

辱 N1	毅 N1	轄 N1	猿 N1
embarrass, humiliate, shame	strong	control, wedge	monkey
zabuniti	jak	kontrolirati	majmun
弦 N1	稔 N1	窒 N1	炊 N1
bowstring, chord, hypotenuse	harvest, ripen	plug up, obstruct	cook, boil
tetiva na luku	Žetva	spriječiti	Kuhanje
洪 N1	摂 N1	飽 N1	冗 N1
deluge, flood, vast	vicarious, surrogate, act in addition to	sated, tired of, bored, satiate	superfluous, uselessness
potop	zamjenički	umoran	prekomjeran
桃 N1	狩 N1	朱 N1	渦 N1
peach tree	hunt, raid, gather	vermilion, cinnabar, scarlet, red, bloody	whirlpool, eddy, vortex
Breskva	lov	cinober	vrtlog
紳 N1	枢 N1	碑 N1	鍛 N1
sire, good belt, gentleman	hinge, pivot, door	tombstone, monument	forge, discipline, train
gospodin	šarka	monument	Forge

N1	N1	N1	N1
刀	鼓	裸	猶
sword, saber, knife	drum, beat, rouse, muster	naked, nude, uncovered, partially clothed	furthermore, still, yet
mač	bubanj	go	osim toga
N1	N1	N1	N1
塊	旋	弓	幣
clod, lump, chink, clot, mass	rotation, go around	bow, bow (archery, violin)	cash, bad habit, humble prefix, gift
grumen	rotacija	nakloniti se	unovčiti
N1	N1	N1	N1
膜	扇	腸	槽
membrane	fan, folding fan	intestines, guts, bowels, viscera	vat, tub, tank
membrana	ventilator	crijevni	PDV
N1	N1	N1	N1
慈	楊	伐	駿
mercy	willow	fell, strike, attack, punish	a good horse, speed, a fast person
milost	vrba	pao	ubrzati
N1	N1	N1	N1
糾	亮	墳	坪
twist, ask, investigate, verify	clear, help	tomb, mound	two-mat area, ~36 sq ft
uganuće	svijetao	grob	Ping

N1	N1	N1	N1
紺	娯	舌	羅
dark blue, navy	recreation, pleasure	tongue, reed, clapper	gauze, thin silk, Rome
plava	rekreacija	jezik	gaza
峡	俸	厘	峰
gorge, ravine	stipend, salary	rin, 1, 10sen, 1, 10bu	summit, peak
ždrijelo	Plaća	Centimetar	vrhunac
圭	醸	蓮	弔
square jewel, corner, angle, edge	brew, cause	lotus	condolences, mourning, funeral
ugao	zakuhati	lotos	saučešće
乙	汁	尼	遍
the latter, duplicate, strange, witty	soup, juice, broth, sap, gravy, pus	nun	everywhere, times, widely, generally
duplikat	sok	kaluđerica	svugdje, posvuda
衡	薫	猟	羊
equilibrium, measuring rod, scale	send forth fragrance, fragrant, be scented	game-hunting, shooting, game, bag	sheep
ravnoteža	mirisan	pucanje	ovca

款 N1 goodwill, article, section, friendship, collusion ugled	**閲** N1 review, inspection, revision pregled	**偵** N1 spy špijun	**喝** N1 hoarse, scold promukao
敢 N1 daring, sad, tragic, pitiful, frail, feeble usuditi se	**胎** N1 womb, uterus utroba	**酵** N1 fermentation kvasac	**豚** N1 pork, pig svinjetina
遮 N1 intercept, interrupt, obstruct presijecati	**扉** N1 front door, title page, front page prednja vrata	**硫** N1 sulphur sumpor	**赦** N1 pardon, forgiveness oprostiti
窃 N1 stealth, steal, secret, private, hushed ukrasti	**泡** N1 bubbles, foam, suds, froth mjehurić	**瑞** N1 congratulations Čestitamo	**又** N1 or again, furthermore, on the other hand osim toga
慨 N1 rue, be sad, sigh, lament velikodušan	**紡** N1 spinning Predenje	**恨** N1 regret, bear a grudge, resentment, malice, hatred žaljenje	**肪** N1 obese, fat debeo

扶 N1	戯 N1	伍 N1	忌 N1
aid, help, assist	frolic, play, sport	5, 5-man squad, file, line	mourning, abhor, detestable, death anniversary
Pomozite	veselje	crta	žalost
濁 N1	奔 N1	斗 N1	蘭 N1
voiced, uncleanness, wrong, nigori, impurity	bustle, run	Big Dipper, 10 sho (vol), sake dipper	orchid, Holland
nečistoća	Trčanje	Kanta	orhideja
迅 N1	肖 N1	鉢 N1	朽 N1
swift, fast	resemblance	bowl, rice tub, pot, crown	decay, rot, remain in seclusion
brzo	sličnost	Zdjela	pokvaren
殻 N1	享 N1	秦 N1	茅 N1
husk, nut shell	receive, undergo, answer (phone), take, get, catch	Manchu dynasty	miscanthus reed
mahuna	podvrći	Dinastija Manchu	miscanthus trska
藩 N1	沙 N1	輔 N1	媒 N1
clan, enclosure	sand	help	mediator, go-between
prilog	pijesak	pomoćni	posrednik

鶏 N1 chicken piletina	**禅** N1 Zen, silent meditation meditacija	**嘱** N1 entrust, request, send a message povjeriti	**胴** N1 trunk, torso, hull (ship), hub of wheel Torzo
迭 N1 transfer, alternation prijenos	**挿** N1 insert, put in, graft, wear (sword) Umetnuti	**嵐** N1 storm, tempest oluja	**椎** N1 oak, mallet hrast
絹 N1 silk Svila	**陪** N1 obeisance, follow, accompany, attend on pozdrav	**剖** N1 divide podijeliti	**譜** N1 musical score, music, note, staff, table, genealogy glazba, muzika
郁 N1 cultural progress, perfume parfem	**悠** N1 permanence, distant, long time, leisure stalnost	**淑** N1 graceful, gentle, pure dobrohotan	**帆** N1 sail jedro
暁 N1 daybreak, dawn, in the event zora	**傑** N1 greatness, excellence veličina	**楠** N1 camphor tree kamforovo drvo	**笛** N1 flute, clarinet, pipe, whistle, bagpipe, piccolo flauta

玲 N1 sound of jewels dragulji	奴 N1 guy, slave, manservant, fellow rob	錠 N1 lock, fetters, shackles zaključavanje	拳 N1 fist šaka
遷 N1 transition, move, change pomicati	拙 N1 bungling, clumsy, unskillful nespretan	侍 N1 waiter, samurai, wait upon, serve Konobar	尺 N1 shaku, Japanese foot, measure, scale, rule mjera
峠 N1 mountain peak, mountain pass, climax vrhunac	篤 N1 fervent, kind, cordial, serious, deliberate žarki	肇 N1 beginning početak	渇 N1 thirst, dry up, parch žeđ
叔 N1 uncle, youth ujak	雌 N1 feminine, female žena	亨 N1 undergo, answer (phone), take, get, catch podvrći	堪 N1 withstand, endure, support, resist Dostojan
叙 N1 confer, relate, narrate, describe savjetovati	酢 N1 vinegar, sour, acid, tart ocat	吟 N1 versify, singing, recital pisati stihove	遞 N1 relay, in turn, sending relej

嶺 (N1)	甚 (N1)	喬 (N1)	崇 (N1)
peak, summit	tremendously, very, great, exceedingly	high, boasting	adore, respect, revere, worship
vrh	vrlo	razmetanje	obožavanje
漆 (N1)	岬 (N1)	癖 (N1)	愉 (N1)
lacquer, varnish, seven	headland, cape, spit, promontory	mannerism, habit, vice, trait, fault, kink	pleasure, happy, rejoice
boja	rt	manirizam	Uživati
寅 (N1)	礁 (N1)	乃 (N1)	洲 (N1)
sign of the tiger, 3-5AM	reef, sunken rock	from, possessive particle, whereupon, accordingly	continent, sandbar, island, country
tigar	greben	iz	Kontinent
屯 (N1)	樺 (N1)	槙 (N1)	姻 (N1)
barracks, police station, camp	birch	twig, ornamental evergreen	matrimony, marry
kasarna	breza	grančica	brak
巌 (N1)	擬 (N1)	塀 (N1)	唇 (N1)
rock, crag, boulder	mimic, aim (a gun) at, nominate, imitate	fence, wall, (kokuji)	lips
stijena	imitirati	ograda	usna

睦 N1	閑 N1	胡 N1	幽 N1
intimate, friendly, harmonious	leisure	barbarian, foreign	seclude, confine to a room
intiman	slobodno vrijeme	varvarin	izdvajati
峻 N1	曹 N1	詠 N1	卑 N1
high, steep	cadet, friend	recitation, poem, song, composing	lowly, base, vile, vulgar
visok	kadet	recitacija	ponizan
侮 N1	鋳 N1	抹 N1	尉 N1
scorn, despise, make light of, contempt	casting, mint	rub, paint, erase	military officer, jailer, old man, rank
prezir	lijevanje	brisanje	Kapetan
隷 N1	禍 N1	蝶 N1	酪 N1
slave, servant, prisoner, criminal, follower	calamity, misfortune, evil, curse	butterfly	dairy products, whey, broth, fruit juice
rob	nesreća	leptir	surutka
茎 N1	帥 N1	逝 N1	汽 N1
stalk, stem	commander, leading troops, governor	departed, die	vapor, steam
proizlaze	zapovjednik	Umrijeti	para

N1 琢	N1 匿	N1 襟	N1 蛍
polish	hide, shelter, shield	collar, neck, lapel	lightning-bug, firefly
polirati	sakriti	ovratnik	svitac

N1 蕉	N1 寡	N1 琉	N1 痢
banana	widow, minority, few	lapis lazuli	diarrhea
banana	Udovica	lazulit	proljev

N1 庸	N1 朋	N1 坑	N1 藍
commonplace, ordinary, employment	companion, friend	pit, hole	indigo
banalan	prijatelj	jama	plava

N1 賊	N1 搾	N1 畔	N1 遼
burglar, rebel, traitor, robber	squeeze	paddy ridge, levee	distant
lopov	Iscijediti	nasip	udaljen

N1 唄	N1 孔	N1 橘	N1 漱
songs with samisen	cavity, hole, slit, very, great, exceedingly	mandarin orange	gargle, rinse mouth
pjevati	rupa	Mandarina	ispiranje

呂 N1	拷 N1	嬢 N1	苑 N1
spine, backbone	torture, beat	lass, girl, Miss, daughter	garden, farm, park
kičma	mučenje	djevojka	vrt
巽 N1	杜 N1	渓 N1	翁 N1
southeast	woods, grove	mountain stream, valley	venerable old man
jugoistok	šuma	dolina	starac
廉 N1	謹 N1	瞳 N1	湧 N1
bargain, reason, charge, suspicion	discreet, reverently, humbly	pupil	boil, ferment, seethe, uproar, breed
pogodba	diskretan	učenik	kuhati
欣 N1	窯 N1	褒 N1	醜 N1
take pleasure in, rejoice	kiln, oven, furnace	praise, extol	ugly, unclean, shame, bad looking
Raduj	peć za sušenje	pohvala	ružan
升 N1	煩 N1	巴 N1	禎 N1
measuring box, 1.8 liter	anxiety, trouble, worry, pain, ill, annoy	comma-design	happiness
mjerna kutija	anksioznost	zarez	sreća

Kanji	Meaning	Croatian
劾 (N1)	censure, criminal investigation	cenzura
堕 (N1)	degenerate, descend to, lapse into	degenerirati
租 (N1)	tariff, crop tax, borrowing	najam
稜 (N1)	angle, edge, corner, power, majesty	rub
桟 (N1)	scaffold, cleat, frame, jetty, bolt (door)	skele
倭 (N1)	Yamato, ancient Japan	japanski
婿 (N1)	bridegroom, son-in-law	mladoženja
斐 (N1)	beautiful, patterned	lijep
罷 (N1)	quit, stop, leave, withdraw, go	Stop
矯 (N1)	rectify, straighten, correct, reform, cure	ispravan
某 (N1)	so-and-so, one, a certain, that person	siguran
囚 (N1)	captured, criminal, arrest, catch	zatvorenici
魁 (N1)	charging ahead of others	punjenje
虹 (N1)	rainbow	duga
鴻 (N1)	large bird, wild goose	guska
泌 (N1)	ooze, flow, soak in, penetrate, secrete	Lučiti
於 (N1)	at, in, on, as for	na
赳 (N1)	strong and brave	hrabar
漸 (N1)	steadily, gradually advancing, finally, barely	postepeno
蚊 (N1)	mosquito	komarac

葵 N1	厄 N1	藻 N1	禄 N1
hollyhock	unlucky, misfortune, bad luck, disaster	seaweed, duckweed	fief, allowance, pension, grant, happiness
slezovača	nesretan	alge	džeparac
孟 N1	嫡 N1	尭 N1	嚇 N1
chief, beginning	legitimate wife, direct descent (non-bastard)	high, far	menacing, dignity, majesty, threaten
početak	Prva supruga	visok	dostojanstvo
凸 N1	暢 N1	韻 N1	霜 N1
convex, beetle brow, uneven	stretch	rhyme, elegance, tone	frost
Konveksan	rastezanje	rima	Mraz
硝 N1	勅 N1	芹 N1	杏 N1
nitrate, saltpeter	imperial order	parsley	apricot
Nitrat	Carski red	peršin	marelica
棺 N1	儒 N1	鳳 N1	馨 N1
coffin, casket	Confucian	male mythical bird	fragrant, balmy, favourable
mrtvački sanduk	konfucijanizam	Feniks	mirisan

慧 N1 wise mudar	**愁** N1 distress, grieve, lament, be anxious nevolja	**楼** N1 watchtower, lookout, high building osmatračnica	**彬** N1 refined, gentle nježan
匡 N1 correct, save, assist ispravan	**眉** N1 eyebrow obrva	**欽** N1 respect, revere, long for poštovanje	**薪** N1 fuel, firewood, kindling gorivo
褐 N1 brown, woollen kimono smeđ	**賜** N1 grant, gift, boon, results potpora	**嵯** N1 steep, craggy, rugged strm	**綜** N1 rule Pravilo
繕 N1 darning, repair, mend, trim, tidy up, adjust štopanje	**栓** N1 plug, bolt, cork, bung, stopper utikač	**翠** N1 green zelena	**鮎** N1 freshwater trout, smelt Som
榛 N1 hazelnut, filbert ljeska	**凹** N1 concave, hollow, sunken konkavan	**艶** N1 glossy, luster, glaze, polish, charm, colorful sjajan	**惣** N1 all svi

蔦 N1	錬 N1	隼 N1	渚 N1
vine, ivy	tempering, refine, drill, train, polish	falcon	strand, beach, shore
loza	temperiranje	Sokol	poduprijeti
衷 N1	逐 N1	斥 N1	稀 N1
inmost, heart, mind, inside	pursue, drive away, chase, accomplish, attain	reject, retreat, recede, withdraw, repel, repulse	rare, phenomenal, dilute (acid)
u većini	progoniti	odbiti	razrijediti
芙 N1	皋 N1	雛 N1	惟 N1
lotus, Mt Fuji	swamp, shore	chick, squab, duckling, doll	consider, reflect, think
lotos	Močvara	Pilence	smatrati
佑 N1	耀 N1	黛 N1	渥 N1
help, assist	shine, sparkle, gleam, twinkle	blackened eyebrows	kindness
pomoći	Sjaj	obrve	ljubaznost
憧 N1	宵 N1	妄 N1	惇 N1
yearn after, long for, aspire to, admire, adore	wee hours, evening, early night	delusion, unnecessarily, without authority	sincere, kind, considerate
diviti	večer	obmana	iskren

脩 N1 dried meat sušeno meso	甫 N1 for the first time, not until samo	酌 N1 bar-tending, serving sake, the host, draw (water) kutlača	蚕 N1 silkworm svilena buba
嬉 N1 glad, pleased, rejoice Raduj	蒼 N1 blue, pale blijed	暉 N1 shine, light sjaj	頒 N1 distribute, disseminate, partition, understand raspodijeliti
只 N1 only, free, in addition samo	肢 N1 limb, arms & legs ud	檀 N1 cedar, sandlewood, spindle tree kedar	凱 N1 victory song pjesma pobjede
彗 N1 comet Kometa	嗣 N1 heir, succeed Nasljednik	叶 N1 grant, answer odgovor	汐 N1 eventide, tide, salt water, opportunity plima
絢 N1 kimono design Predivan	朔 N1 conjunction (astronomy), first day of month veznik	伽 N1 nursing, attending, entertainer dojenje	畝 N1 furrow, 30 tsubo, ridge, rib brazda

N1	N1	N1	N1
抄	爽	黎	惰
extract, selection, summary, copy, spread thin	refreshing, bracing, resonant, sweet, clear	dark, black, many	lazy, laziness
kopirati	osvježavajući	mrak	Lijen
蛮	冴	旺	萌
barbarian	be clear, serene, cold, skilful	flourishing, successful, beautiful, vigorous	show symptoms of, sprout, bud, malt
varvarin	spokojan	cvjeta	izboj, mladica
偲	壱	瑠	允
recollect, remember	I, one	lapis lazuli	license, sincerity, permit
sjetiti se	jedan	lazulit	licenca
蒔	鯉	弧	遥
sow (seeds)	carp	arc, arch, bow	far off, distant, long ago
sjemenke	šaran	luk	daljinski
瑛	附	彪	但
sparkle of jewelry, crystal	affixed, attach, refer to, append	spotted, mottled, patterned, small tiger	however, but
kristal	pričvrstiti	uočen	ali

N1 綺	N1 芋	N1 茜	N1 凌
figured cloth, beautiful	potato	madder, red dye, Turkey red	endure, keep (rain)out, stave off, tide over
lijep	krumpir	crvena boja	podnijeti
N1 皓	N1 洸	N1 毬	N1 婆
white, clear	sparkling water	burr, ball	old woman, grandma, wet nurse
bijela	Mineralna voda	zvr	baka
N1 緋	N1 鯛	N1 怜	N1 邑
scarlet, cardinal	sea bream, red snapper	wise	village, rural community
ljubičastocrven	Morska lešnica	mudar	selo
N1 傲	N1 碧	N1 啄	N1 穰
emulate, imitate	blue, green	peck, pick up	good crops, prosperity
imitirati	zelena	poljubac	usjevi
N1 酉	N1 倹	N1 柚	N1 繭
west, bird, sign of the bird	frugal, economy, thrifty	citron	cocoon
Zapad	štedljiv	limun	larve

亦 N1	詢 N1	采 N1	紗 N1
also, again	consult with	dice, form, appearance, take, coloring	gauze, gossamer
također	savjetovati	kocke	gaza
賦 N1	眸 N1	玖 N1	弍 N1
levy, ode, prose, poem, tribute, installment	pupil of the eye	beautiful black jewel, nine	two, second
regrutovati	oko	devet	dva
錘 N1	諄 N1	倖 N1	痘 N1
weight, plumb bob, sinker	tedious	happiness, luck	pox, smallpox
težina	dosadan	srećom	velike boginje
笙 N1	侃 N1	裟 N1	洵 N1
a reed instrument	strong, just, righteous, peace-loving	Buddhist surplice	alike, truth
trska	jak	stola	Uistinu
爾 N1	耗 N1	昴 N1	銑 N1
you, thou, second person	decrease	the Pleiades	pig iron
vas	smanjenje	Plejade	Mljevenje

莞 N1	伶 N1	碩 N1	宥 N1
reed used to cover tatami	actor	large, great, eminent	soothe, calm, pacify
trska	glumac	veliki	umiriti
滉 N1	晏 N1	伎 N1	朕 N1
deep and broad	late, quiet, sets (sun)	deed, skill	majestic plural, imperial we
duboko	kasno	vještina	ja
迪 N1	綸 N1	且 N1	竣 N1
edify, way, path	thread, silk cloth	moreover, also, furthermore	end, finish
staza	nit	povrh toga	potpun
晨 N1	吏 N1	燦 N1	麿 N1
morning, early	officer, an official	brilliant	I, you, (kokuji)
jutro	Službeno	sjajan	ja
頌 N1	箇 N1	楓 N1	琳 N1
eulogy	counters for things	maple	jewel, tinkling of jewelry
hvalospjev	brojači	javor	dragulj

N1	N1	N1	N1
梧	哉	澪	晟
Chinese parasol tree, phoenix tree	how, what, alas, (question mark)	water route, shipping channel	clear
stablo feniksa	kako	kanal	čisto
衿	凪	梢	丙
neck, collar, lapel	lull, calm, (kokuji)	treetops, twig	third class, 3rd, 3rd calendar sign
vrat	smiriti	grančica	treći
颯	茄	勺	恕
suddenly, smoothly	eggplant	ladle, one tenth of a go, dip	excuse, tolerate, forgive
glatko	patlidžan	kutlača	izgovor
瑚	遵	瞭	燎
ancestral offering receptacle	abide by, follow, obey, learn	clear	burn, bonfire
koraljni	slijediti	čisto	spaliti
虞	柊	侑	謁
uneasiness, fear, anxiety, concern	holly	urge to eat	audience, audience (with king)
strah	božikovina	jesti	publika

N1	N1	N1	N1
斤	嵩	捺	蓉
axe, 1.32 lb, catty, counter for loaves of bread	be aggravated, grow worse, grow bulky, swell	press, print, affix a seal, stamp	lotus
sjekira	nabubri	pritisnite prema dolje	lotos

N1	N1	N1	N1
茉	燿	誼	冶
jasmine	shine	friendship, intimacy	melting, smelting
jasmin	Sjaj	prijateljstvo	Gavun

N1	N1	N1	N1
栞	墾	勁	菖
bookmark, guidebook	ground-breaking, open up farmland	strong	iris
bookmark	njegovati	snaga	iris

N1	N1	N1	N1
椋	叡	胤	凜
type of deciduous tree, grey starling	intelligence, imperial	descendent, issue, offspring	cold, strict, severe
čvorci	inteligencija	potomak	hladno

N1	N1	N1	N1
亥	爵	脹	麟
sign of the hog, 9-11PM	baron, peerage, court rank	dilate, distend, bulge, fill out, swell	Chinese unicorn, genius, giraffe, bright, shining
svinja	baron	proširiti	genije

莉 N1	汰 N1	瑶 N1	瑳 N1
jasmine	luxury, select	beautiful as a jewel	polish
jasmin	luksuzno	dragulj	polirati
耶 N1	椰 N1	絃 N1	丞 N1
question mark	coconut tree	string, cord, samisen music	help
upitnik	Kokos	niz	Pomozite
璃 N1	奎 N1	塑 N1	昂 N1
glassy, lapis lazuli	star, god of literature	model, molding	rise
staklo	zvijezda	Kalup	ustati
柾 N1	熙 N1	菫 N1	諒 N1
straight grain, spindle tree, (kokuji)	bright, sunny, prosperous, merry	the violet	fact, reality, understand, appreciate
žitarica	svijetao	ljubičasta	razumjeti
鞠 N1	崚 N1	濫 N1	捷 N1
ball	towering in a row	excessive, overflow, spread out	victory, fast
lopta	veoma visok	pretjeran	Brz